C000133618

Print culture in

Maynooth Studies in Local History

SERIES EDITOR   Raymond Gillespie

This volume is one of six short books published in the Maynooth Studies in Local History series in 2008. Like their predecessors most are drawn from theses presented as part of the MA course in local history at NUI Maynooth. Also like their predecessors they range widely over the local experience in the Irish past from the middle ages into the twentieth century. That local experience is presented in the complex social world of which it is part. These were diverse worlds that need to embrace such differing experiences as the fisheries of Arklow, or the world of books and reading in Loughrea. For yet others their world was constructed through the tensions which resulted in the murder of Major Denis Mahon near Strokestown in 1847. The local experience cannot be a simple chronicling of events relating to an area within administrative or geographically-determined boundaries since understanding the local world presents much more complex challenges for the historian. It is a reconstruction of the socially diverse worlds of poor and rich, from the poor of pre-Famine Tallaght to the more prosperous world of the Church of Ireland in the diocese of Lismore. Reconstructing such diverse local worlds relies on understanding what the people of the different communities that made up the localities of Ireland had in common and what drove them apart. Understanding the assumptions, often unspoken, around which these local societies operated is the key to recreating the world of the Irish past and reconstructing the way in which those who inhabited those worlds lived their daily lives. As such studies like those presented in these short books, together with their predecessors, are at the forefront of Irish historical research and represent some of the most innovative and exciting work being undertaken in Irish history today. They also provide models which others can follow up and adapt in their own studies of the Irish past. In such ways will we understand better the regional diversity of Ireland and the social and cultural basis for that diversity. If they also convey something of the vibrancy and excitement of the world of Irish local history today they will have achieved at least some of their purpose.

Maynooth Studies in Local History: Number 78

Print culture in Loughrea, 1850–1900

Reading, writing and printing in an Irish provincial town

Bernadette Lally

FOUR COURTS PRESS

Set in 10pt on 12pt Bembo by
Carrigboy Typesetting Services, County Cork for
FOUR COURTS PRESS LTD
7 Malpas Street, Dublin 8, Ireland
e-mail: info@fourcourtspress.ie
http://www.fourcourtspress.ie
and in North America for
FOUR COURTS PRESS
c/o ISBS, 920 N.E. 58th Avenue, Suite 300, Portland, OR 97213.

ISBN 978-1-84682-116-5

Printed in England by
Athenaeum Press Ltd, Gateshead, Tyne & Wear.

Contents

Acknowledgments

I wish to thank some of the people who helped in the completion of this study. I am very grateful to the library staff of Galway County Library, the National University of Ireland, Galway, the National University of Ireland, Maynooth, the National Archives and National Library of Ireland. I would also like to thank my own colleagues in the Galway-Mayo Institute of Technology for all their support. In Loughrea, my grateful thanks to Mrs Anne Monaghan, former owner of Kelly's shop and to Fr Bernard Cuffe, Carmelite Abbey for their assistance. A special thank you to Mr Gerard McInerney for his help.

I thank my supervisor Dr Raymond Gillespie very sincerely for all the help, advice and encouragement.

Finally, I thank my family for all the support and to them, I dedicate this work.

Introduction

The August 1857 issue of the *Loughrea Illustrated Journal* printed a list of articles for sale in Thomas Kelly's 'Book and Stationery Warehouse' in Loughrea. It included perfumery and pills, steel penknives, silver thimbles and violin strings which many shops selling books and stationery also carried, but it is interesting to look at the print and stationery items because they illustrate how print had become part of the normal business of daily life for many people in post-Famine Loughrea. Kelly's list began with an overview of some of the books he stocked. He had 'Bibles, testaments, missals, in variety, every style of binding, classical and mathematical works, books on cookery, domestic economy, gardening, farming and rural affairs' and 'ladies crochet and knitting instructions.'[1] More detailed lists of books appear in other issues of the *Journal*, but this is a general listing, perhaps for the customers not primarily concerned with reading literary works, but interested in the useful information contained in practical manuals on these various topics. For the business community he had 'post, letter, note, foolscap and copy paper' and 'official, adhesive and plain' envelopes. He stocked 'embossed and tinted letter and note paper' for those engaged in correspondence. He had 'mourning and plain visiting cards' for bereavement and social occasions. He also had 'music, marble, glass, sand and blotting paper'. He stocked writing desks and escritoires, ink-stands, plain and fancy sealing wax, 'porcupine-quill, ebony and German-silver penholders' and 'quill-pens, in boxes.' Some of the items are obviously aimed at the gift market but most are the normal necessities of correspondence and business in a world where writing and print were accepted parts of the daily routine. This list illustrates an element of the social, cultural and economic context of print in nineteenth century Loughrea and this short book will attempt a more detailed examination of this theme. Raymond Gillespie, in referring to 17th- and 18th- century Ireland says, by understanding how communities involved with the world of print put printed artefacts to use in daily life 'it is possible to reconstruct something of the social and cultural topographies of those worlds'.[2] In defining print culture, Chartier refers to 'the profound transformation' that a print culture brought to all domains of life, public and private, spiritual and material'.[3] This study will attempt to show how print was received and integrated into Loughrea in the 19th century, at a time when the literacy levels were rising, the provision of education was expanding and the

Printing Establishment,

NEWSPAPER AGENCY OFFICE,
Book and Stationery Warehouse,
LOUGHREA.

THOMAS KELLY,
PROPRIETOR,

HAS FOR SALE THE FOLLOWING ARTICLES :—

Bibles, Testaments, Missals, and Manuals, in variety, every style of binding.

Classical & Mathematical works

Books on Cookery, Domestic Economy, Gardening, Farming, and rural affairs.

Tablets, patent flexible and plain memorandum books.

Ladies' Knitting, Netting and Crochet Instructors.

Post, Letter, Note, Foolscap and Copy Paper.

Official, Adhesive, Plain and black-bordered Envelopes.

Enclosed, Embossed and tinted Letter and Note Paper.

Mourning and plain Visiting Cards.

Music, Marble, Glass, Sand and Blotting Paper.

Pressing and Pasteboards.

Writing Desks and Escritoirs.

Letter Clips and Blotters.

Filtering, Excise and Screw Inkstands

Plain and fancy Sealing-wax.

Quill-Pens, in boxes.

Porcupine-quill, Ebony, and German-silver Penholders.

Fancy and Comic Valentines.

Ribbon Book-markers.

Holloway's Pills and Ointment.

Ivory and Bone Papercutters.

Motto and Initial Seals.

Arnold's and MacDermott's Writing Fluids.

Lessey's Marking Ink.

Superior Shaving Cream.

Brown Windsor and Honey Soap

Razor Strops.

Cloth, Hair, Tooth and Shaving Brushes.

Perfumery.

Rose and Trotter Oil.

Robinson's Liquid Glue.

Brande's Enamel and Tooth-powder.

Beetham's Corn-plaster.

Rodgers's and Barber's Steel Penknives and Scissors.

Silver Thimbles.

Violin Strings and Bows.

Stamped Playing Cards.

Plain and fancy Purses.

Rack-combs.

Ivory and Bone Shirt-studs.

Blue Wax Tapers.

Brill's Patent Night Lights.

Fusees, Vestas and Congreve Matches.

Paint Boxes and Brushes.

Measuring Tapes, &c., with a variety of other articles.

A Constant supply of Room Paper of every description.

1. List of items for sale in Thomas Kelly's shop

availability of print was increasing. It will endeavour to look at the town through a prism of print.

Many works deal with aspects of this study but few treat the whole theme of print culture in a 19th-century Irish provincial town. McClintock Dix[4] in listing surviving early printed material is the obvious starting point. Two works published by the Rare Books Group of the Library Association of Ireland are central to reading on this subject. *Books beyond the pale*[5] contains a valuable article by Vincent Kinnane on the early book trade in Galway. It pertains to Galway city, and does not deal with the county as a whole, but it is useful background material dealing as it does with the reasons for Galway's late arrival on the printing scene. Kevin Whelan's article in the same volume on the dissemination and reception of political literature in the 1790s, although an earlier period than the main focus of this study, looks at the other side of the publishing process, how printed works were received by readers. Reading contexts are explored in the second title, *The experience of reading; Irish historical perspectives*,[6] published in conjunction with the Economic and Social History Society of Ireland. John Logan's article on reading in the national schools and Marie-Louise Legg's piece on the Kilkenny Circulating Library Society were particularly pertinent. Paul Townsend's essay is just one of the interesting articles in *Reading Irish histories*.[7] Townsend examines the role of reading rooms in national movements in 19th-century Ireland, and for Loughrea, where reading rooms feature prominently, this has particular relevance. *The origins of popular literacy in Ireland*[8] edited by Daly and Dickson looks particularly at the decline of the Irish language in the 19th century. Few full monographs have been written on this subject but it is the nature of print culture that it involves many different disciplines. An exception is Niall Ó Ciosáin's *Print and popular culture in Ireland, 1750–1850*[9] which examines the production and use of cheap printed works in Ireland. He uses the study of popular printed literature as a guide to the history of popular culture of the period, a time of transition from a mainly oral to a literate culture. Raymond Gillespie's *Reading Ireland*, treating the 17th and 18th centuries, provides a way of looking at a world through its involvement with the printed word that has influenced the present study. Antonia McManus's, *The Irish hedge school and its books, 1695–1831*,[10] showed the range of printed material available in the hedge schools. Kenneth Milne's study of the Charter schools gave a useful background to those institutions and Akenson's *The Irish education experiment*[11] was a useful source book for the national perspective. Marie-Louise Legg's work on the provincial press, *Newspapers and nationalism*[12] gives an insight into the operation of the newspaper business at local level and highlights its importance as a historical source. *A history of literacy and libraries in Ireland*[13] by Mary Casteleyn also addresses many of the themes of this study. There has been little published on the history of Loughrea but the two volume collection of essays,

The district of Loughrea,[14] provides a thematic approach to Loughrea from 1791 to 1918 and was a valuable source for this study.

This study examines the rise in the use of print and literacy in a 19th-century Irish provincial town. While not much has been published on particular locations, especially small provincial towns, the primary sources exist to make such a study possible. Parliamentary papers provided the primary source material in researching this topic. Printed census reports and the reports of the Registrar General were important sources of literacy data for Loughrea. Various education reports provided information on the state of schools in Loughrea throughout the 19th century, including the earlier Charter school. Two local sources central to this study were the *Loughrea Illustrated Journal* and an unpublished diary of Thomas Kelly, now in private hands in Loughrea. Both sources facilitated a case study of the printing and publishing business of Thomas Kelly, and an examination of the interaction of print with the local community.

Unpublished theses contributed greatly to an understanding of this theme. 'Print for the people: the growth in popular writings and reading facilities in Ireland, 1820–1850'[15] by Mary Feeney provided much valuable and relevant material on reading rooms, newspapers, library facilities and religious publications. Michael Fahy's 'Education in Loughrea and its environs to 1861'[16] was helpful also. 'Schooling and the promotion of literacy in nineteenth-century Ireland'[17] by John Logan is a comprehensive treatment of education with valuable insights into such areas as the measurement of literacy by the use of marriage registration data and the place of the national school system in the growth of a literate population in Ireland.

Loughrea (Baile Locha Riach), a town in east Galway on the main Dublin–Galway road is bordered on the southwest by the lake from which it derives its name. The accepted translation of Baile Locha Riach is 'the town of the grey lake' but John O'Donovan writing in the 1830s disputes this. Referring to the Book of Lecan, he says that the lake was named after Riach, one of the four kings of Maenmach, who drowned in it.[18] The de Burgos founded the town in the early 13th century and for a time Loughrea was the de Burgo seat. Their castle in the town was destroyed in 1580.[19] A tower, part of the walls of the town, survives and is situated close to St Brendan's Cathedral. A Carmelite abbey dating from 1300[20] is bounded on one side by 'the Abbey Walks', a walkway along the old walls and moat of the town. By tradition, the Abbey is the burial place of General St Ruth, slain at the Battle of Aughrim in 1691.[21] Today the town is renowned for St Brendan's Cathedral, built at the turn of the 20th century and regarded as a showcase of the Arts and Crafts movement in Ireland. The cathedral contains stained glass work by Sarah Purser, Evie Hone and Michael Healy, carvings by Michael Shorthall and banners designed by Jack B. Yeats and woven by his sisters, Lily and Elizabeth as part of the Dun Emer Guild.[22] Two figures particularly associated with the building of the cathedral were closely associated with the literary life of Loughrea and also of Ireland, the local curate, Fr Jeremiah O'Donovan and the writer and co-founder of the Abbey Theatre, Edward Martyn. In the post-Famine period of the 19th century the population of Loughrea declined by more than half, from 7,152 in 1841 to 3,260 in 1891.[23] The Famine and post-Famine emigration patterns combined with falling marriage rates were major factors influencing this decline.

Contemporary accounts of Loughrea in the 19th century describe the air of neglect from which the town suffered. Nonetheless it was a considerable market town. Four large fairs were held annually and the *Parliamentary gazetteer* noted 'a large proportion of the agricultural produce of the surrounding country is sold at Loughrea.'[24] The town's geographical position ensured good communication links with Dublin and Galway city and these links improved further when, in 1890, the rail link to Attymon was opened.[25] The second half of the 19th century in Loughrea was a time of striving to reverse the decline. The long campaign to build the rail link is evidence of the attempts made at improvement in the town's condition. The increase in literacy levels and education and the growing number of print based businesses demonstrate how print culture played a vital role in the effort of a community to improve and modernise.

The factors that constitute the development of a print culture in a small town like Loughrea in 19th-century Ireland are examined here from the perspective of demand and supply. The first chapter explores the demand for print in Loughrea in the 19th century. The social and economic structures of post-Famine Loughrea influenced the development of its print culture. A hinterland with a large number of families of the landed gentry and big farms provided a market for the growing number of businesses in Loughrea, including the local bookshop. Conversely, the state of the poor in Loughrea periodically necessitated the distribution of outdoor relief, especially in 1882. A description of the appalling living conditions of labourers in Loughrea towards the end of the century indicates that there was hardly any furniture in the hovels they lived in, let alone books.[26] For these people, print culture had yet to impact on their lives. Yet the desire for literacy manifested itself in the numerous schools operating in Loughrea. The 1826 Parochial Returns[27] list 17 schools within the town varying in standard from a 'good house' to a 'miserable hovel'. The children attending these schools came from all sections of society, their parents recognizing the value of education, however limited its provision. The coming of the national system of education in 1831 standardized the provision of education and made a significant contribution to the rising literacy rates in the second half of the 19th century.

The supply of print in Loughrea in the latter part of the 19th century is the focus of the second chapter. This requires an examination of the growth and diversification of the business community in Loughrea. It shows how print was an integral and essential part of the business life of the town as evidenced by the growth in the postal system, banking and other occupations for which print was fundamental. This chapter also looks at the supply of books available through the school system. The Charter School had a set of rigid guidelines on what reading material was available in their schools and this extended to texts used outside the classroom by pupils who were apprenticed after their time spent in the school. The 17 pay schools of Loughrea had no such restrictions as to the texts used, with the exception of the school run by the London Hibernian Society. Teachers in privately run pay schools used what few books they could afford to purchase from the fees paid by their pupils. The coming of the national schools restricted the texts used to the books produced or approved by the Commissioners for Education. Following on the work started by the Kildare Place Society, the Commissioners produced the texts they deemed necessary for the national school system,. So highly regarded were these texts that they were also used in many schools in England. A criticism levelled at them was that there was an almost complete absence of references to Ireland in these the Irish school books. Irish history, Irish folklore and Irish literature were almost entirely absent from the school texts. One explanation for this lies in the attempt by the Commissioners to avoid sectarian material as these texts were designed for pupils of all denominations within the national school system.

Supply and demand merge in examining the business of the Thomas Kelly of Loughrea. He stimulated demand through his reading room and in the pages of his *Journal* and he fulfilled that demand though his printing business and bookshop. The third chapter is a case study of his printing and publishing business which operated from his Main Street premises in Loughrea for over a century-and-a-half. Kelly's diary shows the range of his printing operation, which included sermons and pastoral works for the clergy, posters and fliers for election candidates, handbills for touring theatre companies and notices for public meetings. He ran the only bookshop in the town, and the lists of works stocked in the bookshop give a valuable insight into the reading of a small provincial town, or at least what was offered for sale. Kelly catered for another aspect of the local print culture by operating a reading room in the town in the 1850s and 1860s. Thomas Kelly also left a remarkable literary and social document in the form of the *Loughrea Illustrated Journal*, a monthly publication he produced from 1857 and which ceased in 1884. No similar journal was published in other towns in the west of Ireland at the time. It is possible that the publication of the *Journal* was influenced in content and format by earlier journals of the 1830s and 1840s such as the *Dublin Penny Journal* or the *Irish Penny Magazine*. They included a similar range of subject matter but those earlier titles had a more Irish focus in their articles. However, the illustration of the Abbey in Loughrea that appears in an 1875 issue of the *Loughrea Illustrated Journal* had already appeared in the *Dublin Penny Journal* of 1834.[28] The *Journal* gives a picture of the town and its inhabitants from the perspective of a man who was constantly striving to improve it. It gives a picture of the literary life of Loughrea. The position of women in that literary life can be assessed through its pages by looking at the types of articles published and the booklists of works stocked in his shop. The *Journal* published works from a group calling itself the Loughrea Female Poetical Society. The Irish language does not feature in the pages of the *Journal*, although Irish texts were stocked in the bookshop. These were mainly school textbooks and reflect the dearth of publishing in the Irish language. Kelly's activities therefore, reflect the growth of print in Loughrea and as such his activities are central to this study.

1. The demand for print in Loughrea

The geographical position of Loughrea, in the east of Co. Galway and on the main Dublin-Galway road, influenced the development of the town's print culture. Travellers, traders, chapmen and ideas had only one route to Galway city from Athlone and Dublin and that was through Loughrea. Regional differences within Co. Galway are marked. In the 19th century, the west of the county differed in many respects from the east where Loughrea is situated. T.P. O'Neill, discussing famine relief in Galway, noted that the situation in Galway, 'particularly in the west of the county', regularly gave cause for concern.[1] The west of the county was more susceptible to the extremes of poverty typically represented in 19th-century travellers' accounts. The east of the county, while suffering greatly during the Great Famine and in receipt of relief at other periods, had a different economic and agricultural basis to the west of the county. Large grassland farms were an 'established feature of the east Connacht plains since the 18th century'[2] and the strongest areas of pastoral farming were the baronies of Loughrea and Ballinasloe. By 1881, Co. Galway had a quarter of the sheep numbers in the country,[3] mostly in the east Galway areas of Loughrea and Ballinasloe. The barony of Loughrea contained a growing number of large farms. In 1860 the agricultural statistics show that there were 10 farms above 500 acres within the barony, 22 by 1880 and 20 by 1899. There were 39 farms in the barony between 200 and 500 acres in 1860. This had increased to 135 by 1880 and was 146 in 1899. This shows a consolidation of farms and this was mainly for the purpose of pasture. Richards points out that a considerable portion of the land in the Loughrea Union was under grass. 56% of the 87% of arable land was under grass in 1893.[4]

Loughrea and its hinterland also displayed marked variations within its social structure. The area around Loughrea was home to many families of the landed gentry. The Blakes of Dartfield and Raford, the Burkes of St Clerens, Marble Hill, Ballydugan and Ballybroder, the Dalys of Dunsandle and Castle Daly were some of the local families whose branches had several substantial houses in the locality. The Smyths of Masonbrook and the Persses of Roxborough were also major landlords. The earls of Clanricarde, although their seat had long since transferred to Portumna, were the principal family in the area. The town was surrounded by a hinterland of sizable farms and landed families who provided a market not only for the latest fashions in Strattons drapery shop in Loughrea but also for the latest publications

2. Map of Loughrea

available in Thomas Kelly's bookshop. Other sections of Loughrea's population shared the appalling poverty levels of the worst of the west of the
county. During the famine crisis of 1879–80, the Loughrea relief committee
distributed between £8,000 and £9,000 of relief in the town.[5] Roger
Richards was part of the Royal Commission on Labour investigation on the
state of agricultural labourers in Ireland. The Union of Loughrea was one of
the four unions he visited. He found that the 'condition of the agricultural
labourer in this union is one of great poverty and wretchedness.'[6] He visited
cottages both in the town of Loughrea and its hinterland. The accom-
modation was unsanitary and filthy. The smoke-filled interiors had little
furniture, light or protection from the elements and he says that although he
was prepared for a marked contrast to the worst of his English experiences,
'the sight of so much squalor and wretchedness, very much of which is
preventable, so disturbed me that I could not sleep.'[7] He did not inspect
cottages other than labourers' cottages, but judging from appearances, they
also seemed to him to be in a similar condition. Earlier descriptions of the
town concur with his observations. The *Parliamentary gazetteer* describing the
town in 1844 says the principal street 'is long, comparatively spacious and
possessed of a large aggregate of tolerably good houses; yet in spite of its
extent, its bustle, and its somewhat urban aspect, it totally fails to relieve the
town from a prevailing character of dinginess, dirtiness and neglect.'[8] This air
of neglect, commented on by other writers also, is often attributed to the
neglect of the town by its landlord, the earl of Clanricarde. Richards notes
that in English districts there were signs of interest taken by the landlord in
the condition of the peasantry, but in the Irish districts it was quite the
exception to find anything of the kind.[9] Hely Dutton, writing almost 70
years before Richards, calls Loughrea a considerable market town with many
respectable families but he too mentions the neglect of the large linen and
yarn hall and of the Mall (Abbey Walks).[10] He also pointed to the benefit of
a resident and interested landlord, the 'cheering influence of the proprietor
on an estate'. 'There is scarcely a possibility of a man of fortune residing on
his own estate without making some kind of improvements.'[11] A constant
theme of the editorials and articles in Thomas Kelly's *Journal* from the late
1850s to the 1880s was the need for improvement in the town's buildings,
walkways, water supplies and industries.

  Between the two extremes of landed gentry and big farmers on one
hand, and the poverty of labourers for whom not enough continuous
employment was available on the other, was a growing middle class of
traders and business people. The demand for literacy and print sprang from
different causes for the different strata of society in the town. The landed
families and gentry had an easier access to a print culture than the less
wealthy sections of society. The big houses had libraries used for education
or decoration. L. Hynes, High St Galway, Book-binding and Circulating

Library, advertised in the *Journal*, books 'bound in every variety of style, to suit either the library or drawing room.'[12] Of course, each family of the landed class was different and took varying levels of interest in books. Lady Gregory tells us there were few books in the Roxborough home of the Persse family, but Dalys of Dunsandle had an exceptional library. Denis Daly of Dunsandle, an MP and friend of Henry Grattan, died in 1791 and his library was auctioned in May 1792. The catalogue for the sale contained 1,450 lots. The library contained two Caxtons and a Chaucer bought at the auction for King George III for £12 10s. 3d. It also included a manuscript of poems in Irish. The sale of his library generated £3,876 14s. 4½d, with many of the volumes going to Trinity College and the King's Inns.[13] Some years earlier in 1779, a ship containing all of Daly's first editions sank off the English coast. 'Gone to edify the fishes off Beachey Head,' he wrote stoically of the loss.[14] The gentry had a greater opportunity to access the culture of print than other strata of society who had neither the money to purchase books, the ability to read them or the circumstances in which to read. Yet for the lower orders, as for all sections of society, the rising literacy levels demonstrates a demand for participation in a print culture. For the poorer sections of society, especially from the 1850s, one incentive to literacy was to prepare for emigration or to read the emigrant letters arriving from England and America. Fortner argues that print communication from emigrants, while not a causal factor, was an important incentive to the growth of literacy.[15] There was also an awareness of the value of literacy and education as a means of self-improvement. For the middle-class businessperson or trader, print was becoming an indispensable tool.

Ó Ciosáin points to economic, political and religious factors stimulating the demands for literacy.[16] The end of the 18th century and start of the 19th century saw the greater frequency and regularity of market transactions within the Irish rural economy setting a higher premium on literacy than before. At the time of the Napoleonic Wars, paper money, even for small denominations like 3s. and 9s., was common making it necessary for small farmers and traders to become literate. Increased commercialization stimulated the growth of literacy of the young, according to Ó Ciosáin, with parents becoming more aware of the importance of literacy for their children and being motivated to ensure that education was provided for them.

People were also becoming more engaged with politics. The influence of newspapers in spreading revolutionary ideas in the final decade of the 18th century has been widely acknowledged. Leonard McNally stated in 1795 that 'every man that can read or hear and understand what is read to him, begins in religion as in politics, to think for themselves.'[17] Other forms of printed matter were also used in the spread of radical political thought. Ballads, broadsheets and pamphlets were produced in great numbers and distributed throughout the country. Arrests were made in Loughrea for the distribution of seditious material. In 1797 Malachy Donelan of the Loughrea Clanricarde Infantry apprehended a man distributing a pamphlet entitled *The duty of armed citizens at this awful period examined.*[18] In 1804 a man named Higgins was arrested in Loughrea for selling biographies of Napoleon.[19] The 19th century saw an increased use of the printed word as a means of politicization. The use of anonymous threatening letters early in the century points to another manifestation of the growing use of literacy. An example of one of these letters from the Loughrea area dates from 1822. It goes as follows: 'I warn all thee Loughray men to all go home or ye shall be rap and bit to pieces and murder and quiter if ye don't go hom Monday.'[20] There is a widely varying degree of literacy displayed in the letters. William Carleton attributed many of these letters to the local schoolmasters but one historian considers that 'most seem to lack much refinement of schooling or practice, and seem to come straight from the soul of some affected, concerned or indeed frantically aggrieved party.'[21] The example from Loughrea would seem to fit into that category. The Young Ireland movement and the *Nation* newspaper used the printed word to great effect for raising political consciousness in the 1840s. The method of distribution of the *Nation* greatly increased the number of its readers. Three hundred copies went to newsrooms and temperance societies and 1,100 copies went to Repeal warders to be read aloud at weekly meetings. The average number of copies distributed for the three-month period up to 31 Dec. 1843 was 10,730. The paper with the next highest circulation for that period was the *Weekly Freeman* with 7,150.[22] Young Irelanders, like the United Irishmen before them, appreciated the value of education and actively supported the teaching of reading. Whelan points to the obvious fact that the 'effectiveness of this propaganda drive depended on a literate populace'.[23] And while the propaganda drive for the United Irishmen found its literate populace in the north-east at the end of the 18th century, much of the rest of the country did not attain those literacy levels until towards the end of the 19th century. Religious factors also played an important role in fuelling the demand for literacy. Presbyterians were obliged to study the Bible and the high literacy rate in the north-east is linked to the religious breakdown of the population and the high proportion of Presbyterians in that part of the country. The high proportion of women who could read and not write points to a religious reason, as the ability to write was not as necessary as the ability to read Scripture.

From 1857 to 1884, Thomas Kelly printed the *Loughrea Illustrated Journal: a monthly miscellany of literature, art, science and local affairs.* The journal contained local information and articles of interest on international affairs, world history and geography, extracts from fiction and poetry. How many of Thomas Kelly's fellow townspeople would have looked forward to the arrival of the latest monthly issue? How many would have been able to read the *Journal*? It is useful to look at how the literacy rates changed in the second half of the 19th century and census data and marriage registration data both help to answer to that question.

John Logan discusses the advantages and disadvantages of the use of signature data in assessing literacy levels.[24] He notes that a signature cannot be taken as anything but the most basic writing ability and that those who can sign their name may not possess any other literacy skill. Also, in itself, it does not indicate any ability in reading. In support of signature data use, he argues that it is clear evidence of the possession of a particular skill and that it is a standard measure enabling comparisons to be made throughout a population. He says 'the ability to sign a document is clear proof that an individual has at the very least acquired skill in writing and inherent in that is the skill of reading – at the very least his or her own name'.[25] It also demonstrates the potential for further growth of the skill level. What is significant about signature data is that it is the only additional measure to add to census data for this period.

An analysis of marriage registration data for the Superintendent Registrars' District of Loughrea, coterminous with the area of the poor law union, on a five-yearly basis from 1865 to 1900 shows a large decrease in the number of people who signed the register with a mark. Of the 254 persons who married in 1865, 113 (44.5%) signed with a mark. 130 persons married in 1900 and 11 (8.5%) of these signed with a mark (table 1).

Table 1 Percentage of persons who signed marriage register with a mark

Census year	Total persons	Total persons signed with mark	% who signed with a mark
1865	254	113	44.5
1870	226	99	43.8
1875	178	38	21.3
1880	90	32	35.6
1885	120	30	25.0
1890	150	38	25.3
1895	168	29	17.3
1900	130	11	8.5

Source: *Reports of the Registrar General, 1865–1900*

It is the percentage decrease, from 44.5% to 8.5% in the numbers signing with a mark that is significant, as the actual number of persons marrying had decreased from 254 to 130, a decrease of 48.8%. This reflects a decrease in the population in the Superintendent Registrar's District of Loughrea from 29,139, the 1865 figure from the 1861 census, to 22,244 (1891 census) in 1900, a decrease of 23.6%. A population decrease of 23.6% does not fully account for a decrease in the marriage rate of 48.8 per cent. The marriage rate was decreasing in Ireland since the Famine and was lowest in Co. Galway. The Registrar General's report for 1885 states that the rate of marriage in Galway and Mayo was the lowest in the country, at 2.8 per 1000, compared to the highest of 6.8 per 1000 in Dublin.[26] The report of 1880 states that 'the low marriage rate in Ireland, as compared with other countries, must be largely attributable to the extensive emigration which takes place among persons of marriageable age.'[27] It is interesting to note that *Slater's Directory* of 1870 lists a Patrick McCarthy as 'emigration agent' in Loughrea.[28] Thomas Kelly and his nephew, Michael, also acted as agents for passenger shipping companies. The report also points out that there is likely be a deficit in Catholic marriage numbers as some were not registered but this is not measurable. The marriages in Loughrea district were at their lowest point in 1885 when 60 marriages took place. The number increased in 1890 and 1895 to 75 and 84 respectively, but decreased again in 1900 to 65.

The Registrar General's reports on marriage data are separated into religious groupings. It does not however give data for individuals of a particular denomination who signed with a mark. However, in Loughrea, the vast majority of the marriages were conducted between Roman Catholics. In 1865, of the 127 marriages, only 4 were Church of Ireland. In 1900, of the 65 marriages, only 2 were Church of Ireland. In 1875, 1880 and 1890, only Roman Catholic marriages were recorded.

The numbers of men and women signing the marriage register with a mark are largely similar from 1865 to 1895 when a gap between men and women emerges (see table 2). In 1865, 42.5% of men and 46.5% of women signed with a mark. By 1895 the gap between men and women widens significantly with 22.6% of men and 11.9% of women signing with a mark and in 1900, 13.8% of men and 3.1% of women signed with a mark.

**Table 2 Percentage of men and women signing
marriage register with a mark**

Year	Marriages	% Men	% Women
1865	127	42.5	46.5
1870	113	42.5	45.1
1875	89	20.2	22.5
1880	45	31.1	40.0
1885	60	23.3	26.7
1890	75	25.3	25.3
1895	84	22.6	11.9
1900	65	13.8	3.1

Source: *Reports of the Registrar General, 1865–1900*

Additional evidence on literacy rates is provided by the 19th-century censuses. Thomas Larcom was one of the three commissioners appointed to conduct the 1841 census and it was his aim to produce 'a social survey, not bare enumeration'.[29] To this end, literacy rates were included in the 1841 census and they continued to be recorded until 1911. The three categories of 'read and write', 'read only' and 'illiterate' were the categories used. The 1851 census separates the population of public institutions from the rest of the population. This is the only census to do so during the period under review, most likely because the numbers in the institutions were so large at this time following the Famine. This was the case with the workhouse in Loughrea, by far the largest of the public institutions in the town. The workhouse in Loughrea was opened in 1842 and was built to accommodate 800 paupers, but for 1849 the numbers remained between 2,000 and 3,000. The highest number was in February 1849 when it housed 2,876 inmates.[30] By 1851, the number had not diminished greatly as the census records it at 2,691. The total population for the parish, excluding the public institutions, was 4,519 giving a total population of 7,210. Therefore, 37.3% of the population was in the Workhouse.

Analyzing the census data is not without its difficulties. The 1841, 1851, and 1861 censuses give the literacy figures, excluding the under-5s. The 1871, 1881, and 1891 census gives the literacy figures inclusive of all ages and also breaks them down to different age groups. Unfortunately, the first category is the under-7s and not under-5s. For the purpose of comparing the literacy rates from 1841 to 1891, I have added the numbers of the under-5s to the 'Neither read nor write' column. In the under-7s category, there are numbers who can read and write, for example in 1891, 28 could read and write and 41 could read. To exclude the under-7s category and compare it to the earlier returns, which exclude the under-5s, does not appear to give the true picture. For this reason, I have added the under-5s to the illiterate group, calculating that it is very unlikely that many, if any, would have had literacy skills.

Table 3 Percentage who could read and write – Loughrea Parish

Census year	Total	Read and write	% read & write
1841	7152	1877	26.2
1851	7210	2118	29.4
1861	4001	1466	36.6
1871	3699	1547	41.8
1881	3673	1911	52.0
1891	3260	2053	63.0

Source: *Census Data, 1841–1891*

The figures show that the proportion of the population who could read and write in Loughrea in the second half of the 19th century rose considerably (table 3). While the actual rise from 1,877 to 2,053 is only an increase of 176, the percentage of those able to read and write rose from 26.2% in 1841 to 63% in 1891, an increase of 36.8%. The striking figure is the decrease in the overall population, from 7,152 to 3,260, a decrease of 54.4% between 1841 and 1891. The large numbers, 2,691, in the Loughrea workhouse, accounts for the continued high population in 1851. As the workhouse did not open until 1842, the high population for 1841 is not a distorted figure for Loughrea parish.

The proportion of those who could read only was a low figure of 11.5% in 1841 and reduced to 6.9% by 1891, so the isolated skill of reading without writing was obviously limited throughout the period (table 4).

Table 4 Percentage who could read only – Loughrea Parish

Census year	Total	Read only	% read only
1841	7152	819	11.5
1851	7210	940	13.0
1861	4001	420	10.5
1871	3699	484	13.1
1881	3673	355	9.7
1891	3260	225	6.9

Source: *Census Data, 1841–1891*

The proportion of the population who could neither read nor write halved during the period 1841 to 1891 (see table 5). It went from 4,456 (62.3%) to 982 (30.1%). What is striking about this figure is that by 1891 there was still such a high proportion of the population of the parish, 30.1%, who were not part of an increasingly literate world. This figure is however in line with the county levels of literacy. The percentage for Co. Galway of illiterates was 33.9% in 1891 falling from 62.9% in 1861.[31]

Table 5 Percentage who could neither read nor write

Census year	Total	Neither read nor write	% neither read nor write
1841	7152	4456	62.3
1851	7210	4152	57.6
1861	4001	2115	52.9
1871	3699	1668	45.1
1881	3673	1407	38.3
1891	3260	982	30.1

Source: *Census Data, 1841–1891*

It is interesting to compare the census literacy figures with the marriage registration data discussed above.

Table 6 Comparison of census and marriage registration data

Census Year	% who could neither read nor write	Marriage registration year	% who signed with a mark
1841	62.3	1865	44.5
1851	57.6	1870	43.8
1861	52.9	1875	21.3
1871	45.1	1880	35.6
1881	38.3	1885	25.0
1891	30.1	1890	25.3
		1895	17.3
		1900	8.5

Source: *Census Data, 1841–1891, Registrar General's Reports, 1865–1900*

Table 6 shows that in 1861 the census records that 52.9% of the parish were illiterate, in 1865, 44.5% signed the Marriage Register with a mark. In 1881, census figures reduced the illiteracy rate to 38.3%, while the 1880 Registrar's

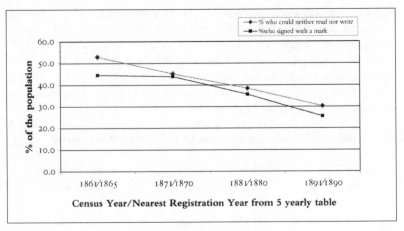

3. Comparison of census and marriage registration literacy data for Loughrea

Source: *Census data 1861–1891, Registrar-General's Reports, 1865–1890*

report states that 35.6% signed with a mark. There is a correlation between the two sets of data and both show a similar percentage decrease in illiteracy levels. The 1890 Registration percentage at 25% is close to the census figure of 30.1% (fig. 1).

By 1901 the percentage of illiterates in Loughrea (Urban) District Electoral Division was actually 13.6%. (By the 1901 Census, the District Electrical Divisions had replaced the parish as the unit for measuring literacy rates, thus making comparisons with earlier censuses difficult for the smaller territorial divisions.) In a national context, Loughrea fitted into national trends. The percentage of people illiterate in the country as a whole was 53% in 1841 and 18% in 1891, but in Co. Galway, it was still as high as 33.9% in 1891.

The 1901 Census is a remarkable tool for profiling literacy. By taking census returns from a sample of streets in Loughrea, we can see what proportion of the population of that street was illiterate and also their age, sex, religion and occupation. Looking at four streets in Loughrea town, Abbey Lane, Athenry Road, Bride Street and Main Street, we can see that of a total of 518 persons over the age of fifteen, 56 (11%) were illiterate. This number includes eight persons who stated they could 'read only'. The proportion of those illiterate varied from street to street. Main Street had 65 households and a total of 218 persons over the age of fifteen. Of those, nine (4%) were illiterate. Athenry Road had a total of 16 households with 51 persons over the age of fifteen. Of those, 11 (21%) were illiterate. This is a much higher proportion than Main Street. It has to be remembered that

Main Street was the principal business street in the town and was likely to have a population of a higher socio-economic level than Athenry Road. As it was the main business street, many of those filling in the census owned the businesses but also many of those who were employed in the businesses also lived on the premises. For example, the return for the Stratton household includes five family members plus four employees; a drapers assistant, a dressmaker, a milliner and a domestic servant, all of whom were literate.

Females constituted a higher proportion of the illiterate population than men. Of the 56 illiterate, 34 were female as opposed to 22 male. The age profile is also interesting to look at, 35 of the 56 were 50 years of age and over. By the end of the 19th century literacy was a prerequisite for engagement with business life, a topic explored further in this chapter. It is interesting therefore to consider the occupations of those classed as illiterate in the sample area of Loughrea. Of the 34 females classed as illiterate, 13 are categorized as wife or widow with no other occupation. Four of those were married to general labourers. The occupations of other husbands of illiterate wives included mason, car man, pedlar, shoemaker and army pensioner. Twelve illiterate women are listed as servant or domestic servant. Other occupations of illiterate women are seamstress, washerwoman and housekeeper and pensioner. There is also one shopkeeper and one merchant. Closer examination of these two returns shows that other family members who were literate were involved in those businesses. Among the 22 men classed as illiterate, nine were general labourers. There were two farmers and two servants. Other occupations were a mason, car man, baker, painter and also one publican. As the vast majority of the population of Loughrea was Roman Catholic, it is no surprise that this is also reflected in the literacy figures. All those listed as illiterate in the four streets examined were Catholic except for one Church of Ireland woman. The person in question was 80 years old and would have been just 10 years of age at the introduction of the national education system in 1831 and was perhaps just too old to avail of it.

Overall, the census returns of 1901 show that those classed as illiterate were generally wives or female servants and male labourers and were 50 years of age and over. They were also more likely to live in poorer sections of the town. The link between literacy and socio-economic status is evident even from this small sample. A similar analysis of the whole town would uncover the unique social geography of Loughrea at the turn of the century.

Table 7 Literacy figures for four Loughrea streets – 1901 Census

Street	Number of households	Persons over 15 years	Read & write	Illiterate	% illiterate
Abbey Lane	41	112	93	19	17
Athenry Road	16	51	40	11	21
Bride Street	43	137	120	17	12
Main Street	65	218	209	9	4
Totals	165	518	462	56	11

Source: *Census Report 1901*

There is a reciprocal relationship between the rise of literacy and the development of print culture. The rise in the rates of literacy demonstrates, and leads to, a demand for the printed word and the printed word needs a literate population. Rising literacy rates increased the demand for print in all its forms. Literacy rates rose after the introduction of the national system of education but the fact is that a large percentage of the population had acquired reading and writing skills prior to 1831. The presence of a substantial number of farmers and landed gentry around Loughrea together with a growing business community in the town ensured a market for printed material in Loughrea. That market was not evenly distributed throughout the population and many in the town, for economic reasons, were not in a position to engage with a print culture. But the rising literacy levels ensured a wider distribution of the ability to read among all classes of society and created a demand for print. How that demand manifested itself and was satisfied will be examined in the following chapter. J.R.R. Adams observes that, because of the proliferation of cheap reading material in the latter half of the 19th century, the three requisites of a mass reading public were 'increased literacy, leisure and a little pocket money'.[32] By the turn of the 20th century Loughrea had reduced its illiteracy rate from over 60% in 1841 to 30% in 1891. The social conditions of the time did not afford much leisure and pocket money was scarce, but Loughrea was on the way to achieving the status of a literate society.

2. The supply of print in Loughrea

Loughrea was only a decade behind Galway city in having a local printer established in the town. It was thus in a position to supply printed material from within the town, adding to what was supplied from external sources. Connacht was poorly supplied with print, 'possibly owing to its low levels of commercialization and scattered population which made it difficult to market books in the hinterland of Galway' according to Gillespie.[1] The first evidence of printing in Galway dates from 1754. W.G. Wheeler considers it a mystery in the history of Irish provincial printing that Galway, such a 'comparatively large and ancient town with long established corporate institutions should not have attracted a printer before 1754.'[2] Kinane[3] offers possible solutions to this mystery. He points to geographic and economic reasons to explain Galway's late embrace of printing. The 18th-century spread of print to the provinces coincided with a down turn in Galway's trading economy. The wine trade had collapsed and the number of ships visiting the port dropped from 30 to 35 in the early part of the century to 19 in 1760. The poor conditions of the county's road system made internal communications difficult. The Dublin–Galway road was suitable for coaches only as far as Athlone as late 1709. The linguistic makeup of the population was another factor militating against the introduction of print. The majority of the population was Irish-speaking and only a fraction of the printing work at the time was in the Irish language. The highest illiteracy rates were within the Irish speaking population.

The first evidence of printing in Loughrea recorded by E.R. McClintock Dix is 1766. It is likely that the printer, John Reynolds, was working in Loughrea for some time prior to that date, as the surviving fragment is for an ambitious project unlikely to be undertaken without some experience of the trade. A folio found in a volume of the Stowe MSS in the Royal Irish Academy consists of a proposal for a work to be published entitled 'An historical and genealogical dissertation on the origins of the chief septs of the old Scoto-Milesian and Strongbonian races in Ireland'. It is dated '12 July 1766' and contains the imprint 'Loughrea, Printed by John Reynolds'. The four-page folio contains the title information on page 1, page 2 is blank, page 3 contains conditions of subscription and page 4 has 21 names to whom subscriptions may be paid throughout the country. One of the conditions of subscription states that the volume would be 'quarto in size, of about 400 pages, good type, excellent paper and well bound and lettered on the back'. The price for subscribers was half a guinea, half to be paid on subscription and half on delivery. Non-subscribers were to pay 13s. 6d. It is not known whether the work was ever published but it does show that a printer was established and working in Loughrea at that date. Dix remarks that the 'enterprise shown by Reynolds, in this small town, is remarkable for the period.'⁴ Not everybody appreciated his enterprise however as the following advertisement appears in the Cork publication, *Flyn's Hibernian Chronicle* on 22 November 1773, 'Five guineas reward. Ran away, on Saturday night, the 6th instant, from the service of John Reynolds, Printer, in Loughrea, Arthur Neal and James Farrell.'⁵ Reynolds was also the printer of the first known Loughrea newspaper, *The Connaught Mercury or Universal Register*. Fragments of this publication were found dating from 1770 and 1772 but Dix estimates that it probably started in 1765 or 1769, as 'Vol 111' was printed on one of the fragments. Dix points out, as do Ó Ciosáin,⁶ Wheeler⁷ and other writers on the subject, that one of the major difficulties of the study of early printing, is that so little survives and what does is often by chance. Dix observed that if the fragments of this newspaper had not survived, its existence would not be known. He noted that 'it is another instance of the painful fact that, in so many cases, provincial printing has literally vanished.'⁸

L. Conway published another newspaper, the *Connaught Gazette* dating from 1797, in Loughrea. Little is known of printing activity in Loughrea until 1824 when P.B. Richardson, Main Street, is listed as a printer in *Pigot's Directory*.⁹ Reprints of a poem about Loughrea, originally published by Richardson, appeared in the *Loughrea Illustrated Journal*.¹⁰ The piece is introduced as follows: 'We have been kindly favoured by a friend with a small pamphlet, composed and printed in this town, in the year 1834, by Mr. P.R. Richardson from which we will make a few extracts'. The implication that the piece is written, as well as printed, by Richardson is borne out by the content of the piece, a long poem, which ends:

> Despoiled of fortune, commerce, health and fame,
> Thy former wealth Loughrea, is but now a name,
> And we 'of the Press' – with our prattling care,
> Of disappointments sad – have got a share;
> As grief, with adverse winds, we can't control
> We must have hope – that anchor of the soul
> None can tell what Providence means to do
> Or what great change Jehovah has in view
> Oh! May we yet rejoice, in songs of praise,
> Forget the past and welcome better days.¹¹

Provincial printing in Ireland declined from the middle of the 19th century. Improved road and rail communication facilitated the easier transport of printed material from Dublin. Schoolbooks were being sourced centrally from Dublin. Wheeler considers that the higher wages in Dublin would have enticed qualified printers to the capital where a journeyman in 1850 would earn 31s. per week compared to the Cork rate of 23s. or 13s. to 14s. in Sligo.[12] Provincial printers after the mid-century specialized in jobbing printing work such as posters, labels, handbills, religious tracts and Catholic pastorals. They usually were the retail outlet for their own work and were booksellers and stationers. Thomas Kelly, printer, bookseller and stationer in Loughrea fits this profile and could be categorized merely as a jobbing printer were it not for the fact that he was also responsible for the *Loughrea Illustrated Journal*. Kelly first appears in the trade directories in 1848 but had been working as a printer in Loughrea since at least 1838. A privately published booklet, *On the necessity of reforming the religious orders in Ireland*, printed by Kelly bears that date.

In early 19th-century Ireland many types of printed material were in short supply. Printed religious matter, however, was commonplace. Between 1836 and 1840, an estimated 40,000 moral and religious books were distributed by the Catholic Society of Ireland.[13] The Religious Tract and Book Society for Ireland between 1810 and 1843 had published and distributed over 9,000,000 works: 7,000,000 tracts and 2,000,000 books.[14] Loughrea could hardly have escaped from this avalanche of print. Mr Daly of Castle Daly was given a well-thumbed copy of Charles Walmesley's *General history of the Christian church*, commonly known as the 'prophesies of Pastorini', to read in a Loughrea inn in 1822.[15] But there were other sources for print in Loughrea. First, the reading rooms, which appeared at various times throughout the 19th century, were a focus outside the home and school where reading was the principal activity. Secondly, the newspaper was a vital source of local, national and international information and was a medium of print which expanded greatly in the second half of the 19th century. No local newspapers were produced in Loughrea in the period but there was access to other local titles from Galway and Tuam which spanned the period. The *Tuam Herald* began in 1837 and continues to date; the *Galway Vindicator* was published from 1841 until 1899, the *Galway Express* from 1853 until 1920. For children, reading material, however incomplete, was provided through the school system. And finally, by the end of the 19th century, print and literacy were essential components of running a business and of the economic life of a town.

The Temperance movement was established in the late 1830s by Fr Theobald Mathew to instil sobriety into the Irish character, but it was also 'a campaign for the social revival of the Irish people, as much as a mass crusade against alcohol.'[16] The establishment of reading rooms was integral to the

Temperance societies. 'We have not only bad appetites to contain, but great faculties to cultivate,' declared Charles Gavin Duffy.[17] The thirst that must be cultivated was a thirst for knowledge and reading rooms were to help satisfy that thirst. In August 1840, the Loughrea Temperance Society ran a fundraising event, the receipts of which were to be 'applied to the establishment of a library, and the purchase of useful and valuable books for the society.'[18] The Temperance Society in Loughrea lasted longer than the majority of Temperance Societies as most had disappeared by the time of the Famine. It is also possible that there were revivals of the society throughout the period and that it was not constantly active. In 1875, the Loughrea Temperance Society was making plans to establish 'a night-school for the benefit of the juvenile members of the institution.'[19] In 1876, Thomas Kelly noted in the *Journal*, that 'the Librarian of the Temperance Library acknowledged the donations of five volumes of *Thiers history of the consulate and empire* and other valuable works from Mrs Stratton and a large number of interesting magazines from Mr William Shadwell of Loughrea.'[20] *Slater's Directory* for 1881 refers to a Temperance reading room in Loughrea whose secretary was Peter Sweeney.[21]

The Repeal Association saw the success of the Temperance reading rooms and adopted the model to suit their purposes. They wanted reading rooms to educate the people in the history and culture of the country and to raise political consciousness. The Repeal Association in Loughrea was active in the 1840s and a Repeal reading room was established in the town. Rules for the establishment of reading rooms had been adopted by the Repeal Association in January 1845. These were published in the *Tuam Herald* in January 1845.[22] The *Tuam Herald* referring to Loughrea in February 1845, noted that 'the Repeal reading room was long looked forward to' and that 'a large room has been taken in Church Lane, the most central that could be had, and will be open to the public on Sunday next, where a meeting of the Repealers will take place.'[23] Later that year the reading room had obviously moved to Bride Street, as a dispute over the location was appealed to the Association and the room was moved from Bride Street to a more central location.[24] The Loughrea Repeal reading room was one of those who opposed deleting the *Nation* newspaper from its subscriptions when the Young Irelanders split from the O'Connellite faction.[25] Writing in 1893 to the newly formed 'Loughrea Social and Literary Club', Mr Henry Smyth wrote of a 'Literary Institute way back in the forties which boasted the possession of a reading room and a few books'. It was in 'the third house from Abbey Lane on the Main Street side then occupied by Mr Jas. Young, who acted as Librarian, Bookbinder and Custodian'[26] James Young is listed in *Slater's Directory* for 1846 as a boot and shoe maker, not an occupation usually linked to literary affairs, but the Repeal reading rooms were formed out of a political, not literary, ideology and arguably attracted a wider

THE

Loughrea Illustrated Journal,

A Miscellany of

LITERATURE, LOCAL AFFAIRS, &c.

THE LOUGHREA ABBEY.

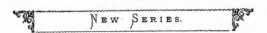

NEW SERIES.

LOUGHREA: THOMAS KELLY, PRINTER AND PUBLISHER.

4. Cover of *Loughrea Illustrated Journal*

support because of this. It may also demonstrate how print and the practice of reading was moving out from the stratum of society previously accustomed to it and reaching into wider social and cultural circles. Temperance and Repeal reading rooms demonstrated how print and the ideas conveyed through print could be disseminated and were a means of meeting the growing demand for printed material.

The tradition of reading rooms continued with Thomas Kelly's reading room which was active in Loughrea in the late 1850s and early 1860s. His diary for the years 1858 to 1863 mentions some of its subscribers; 15 names are mentioned for 1858 but his diary is not a complete listing. The gentry and businessmen of the town made up the majority of the membership. Mr Stratton, draper, and Mr T. Macklin, owner of a hardware business, were members, as was Mr James Smyth of Masonbrook. Colonel Crispen and the County Inspector, Mr P. Hobart were also members. Eight subscriptions are listed in 1859 and none for the following years although the reading room itself is mentioned. In January 1860 he wrote that a 'list is posted in the reading room'.[27] In 1862 he noted that the reading room has been 'papered and painted this week by a painter from Ennis.'[28] In some of the entries he stated that the subscriber had been proposed by a third party, presumably another member. 'J.H. Blake pays 10s. a year subscription to the Reading Room from 1st inst. and he is proposed a member by Mr Robert Burke.'[29] The reading room was also used as a venue for public meetings. Kelly writes, 'a meeting was held in the reading room on Saturday night, to mark another effort to establish Town Commissioners, deputation to wait on Mr Blake at the office.'[30] Mr Blake was the agent to Lord Clanricarde, who also a subscriber to the reading room. While the reading rooms of the 1840s originated in religious and political movements, Thomas Kelly's Reading Room of the 1850s and 1860s did not appear to have a political or religious basis. His diary for that period does not indicate a religious or political bias, nor does the membership reflect it. A reading room with Lord Clanricarde and Colonel Crispin of the local militia among its members was unlikely to have been set up under the Repeal Association. It is more likely that Kelly's reading room catered for small numbers of the local gentry and businessmen of the town. It is possible that 'news room' rather than 'reading room' is a more appropriate name. There is no reference in his diary to books in the reading room, although there are numerous references to its newspapers.

In 1892 a Loughrea Social and Literary Club was established in the town. The purpose of this short-lived club was to encourage the study of Irish literature and to 'afford its members the facility to become acquainted with the great work of Irish writers'. It was also to provide 'wholesome and instructive reading matter from the newspapers, periodicals and magazines of the day.'[31] The club had up to 40 members and subscribed to daily and evening newspapers including *Evening Herald, Evening Telegraph, Tuam News* and *United Ireland* and also the *Review of Reviews, Irish Monthly* and *Chambers Monthly*.[32] It became affiliated to the Irish National Literary Society from which it received a consignment of 50 books as a contribution towards its library. Its main public event was the organizing of a lecture in Loughrea by Maud Gonne MacBride, nationalist activist and founder of Inghinidhe na hÉireann, in April 1893. It was also involved in organizing Irish classes. It is ironic that a society, which did not include women as members, should have a woman as principal speaker at its main public event. There is no record of the Club after 1895. It is, however, another example of people coming together to provide material to read and a space in which to do it. A further example appeared in 1900 with Fr O'Donovan's Society. Fr Jeremiah O'Donovan, later known as the writer Gerald O'Donovan, was the Roman Catholic curate in Loughrea from 1896 to 1904 when he departed for England and subsequently resigned his ministry. He was a central figure in the cultural revival movement and was involved with the co-operative movement with Count Plunkett, the Gaelic League and the Irish literary revival. He was a regular guest of Edward Martyn at his home in Tulira Castle.[33] In 1900, he founded St Brendan's Total Abstinence Society in rooms rented in the military barracks. The society had a large membership of up to 300 men, and carried out an impressive range of activities. It included a recreation room with modern facilities and a gymnasium. It also included a library with what was described as a 'valuable collection of books'. Douglas Hyde delivered a lecture to the Society, classes in Irish language and music were delivered and a chapter of Joyce's *History of Ireland* was read before its weekly meetings.[34] When O'Donovan left Loughrea in 1904, the Society was still flourishing. The society and its library was part of O'Donovan's belief in the concept of village libraries. O'Donovan, with the co-operative movement founder and writer, George Russell (Æ), were driving forces in the movement for promoting village libraries under the auspices of the Irish Agricultural Organisation Society. The first library was set up under the Irish Agricultural Organisation Society by the Tissara Agricultural Society in Co. Roscommon in 1899 with 80 books. The basis of the book selection was a list of 100 titles chosen by O'Donovan. Within a short time this library had 75 members and a stock of 128 volumes. The most popular titles were *The story of Ireland* by A.M. Sullivan, Kickham's *Knocknagow* and *Ireland's schools and scholars* by Dr John Healy.[35] George Russell was an enthusiastic supporter of the village library idea but had a broader view of the type of literature that should be made available there. He advocated 'good libraries of Anglo-Irish literature and of the best books of the world'.[36] Although part of the Irish literary revival, he did not believe that the reading material should be exclusively Irish. By 1904, up to 50 libraries had been established and some of them continued until they were brought under the public library structure in 1925.[37]

The reading rooms of the 19th century were about the provision of reading spaces and material, but the reading of newspapers could take place in almost every context. Writing in 1835 near Tuam on his journey in Ireland, Alexis de Tocqueville asked his guide, the local priest, what the group of peasants gathered at the school door were doing. He was told that they were gathered to hear the newspaper read to them by the local teacher.[38] The image of the group listening to the newspaper being read aloud is a familiar one in 19th-century Ireland. Legg emphasizes the importance of the local press. She concludes that the increase in the number of newspapers following the abolition of taxes in 1855 and the sharp reduction in their price gave a spur to the expression of nationalist ideas.[39] They were read for other reasons too, for important local information and reports of local events. Thomas Kelly remarks in his diary, 'The papers in great demand, they contain proceedings in Ballinasloe.'[40] The event referred to was the consecration of the chapel in Ballinasloe which Cardinal Wiseman and Dr John MacHale attended. Newspapers also brought vital weather and crop condition reports for a readership where the Famine was a very recent memory. 'The papers mention the rapid spread of the disease in several parts of Ireland, this locality pretty free,'[41] Kelly noted. Newspapers were the only source of information on world happenings and news of a major war would always increase sales. 'The papers bring intelligence of great battle between the French and the Austrians – 20,000 of the latter killed or wounded,'[42] writes Kelly in his diary and 'Great demand for papers owing to the news from the war.'[43] Kelly's brief diary entries give a contemporary reaction to events as seen from the newspapers.[44]

There is little evidence of the scale of newspaper sales in Loughrea but we know that at one point Kelly was getting one dozen '*M. J. News* and 1½ doz *M. J. Freeman*.'[45] He was also selling the *Times* and on at least one occasion it arrived late to the reading room. The '*Times* comes to the Reading Room by midday mail instead of morning mail' he notes in his diary. On another occasion, deliveries are mixed up and the '*Freeman's* 1½ doz came by Athenry instead of Woodlawn.'[46] Local newspapers carried articles relating to Loughrea and were undoubtedly available for sale in the town. The *Tuam Herald*, started in 1837 and the *Galway Vindicator* running from 1841 to 1899, were two of the longest running and most popular of the local newspapers. The *Galway Vindicator* reviewed works available in Kelly's bookshop and the *Tuam Herald* covered news items from Loughrea throughout the period. The short-lived *Loughrea Nationalist*, which ran for some months in 1905, was actually produced in Ballinasloe.

The upper levels of society always had easier access to print than the less privileged. Even in the early 17th century, the earl of Clanricarde could have merchants purchase books for him in Lisbon[47] and assembled a private library. Dalys of Dunsandle had a substantial library. Not all the gentry shared a similar interest in books and libraries. Roxborough House, just three miles from Loughrea, was home to the young Augusta Persse and was sadly short of reading material. Her mother did not 'consider book learning as of any great benefit to girls.'[48] But each Christmas, a box of books would arrive for the children to choose from. She describes the effect of receiving the two volumes of Chambers' *Encyclopaedia of English literature*, as 'the breaking of a new day, the discovering of a new dawn.'[49] She was also discovering the ballads and stories of the Gaelic past and remembered standing on tiptoe at the counter of the little Loughrea bookshop purchasing the *The harp of Tara* and *The Irish song book*. She quotes the 'old bookseller' saying, 'I look to Miss Augusta to buy all my Fenian books'.[50] She was subsequently given a copy of *The spirit of the nation*, 'a shilling copy, bound in green cloth'. She does not say if this was from the same Loughrea bookshop, but it was a title stocked by Kelly's Bookshop.

For many, exposure to books only occurred in school and the ethos of the school dictated the type of reading material available. The Charter Schools were established in Ireland in 1733 as a 'means of converting and civilizing the Irish natives and in which the children of the poor might be instructed gratis in the English tongue, and the fundamental principles of true religion and loyalty.'[51] Lord Clanricarde provided an annuity towards the support of a school in Loughrea and this was established in 1750 under his patronage. The Loughrea Charter School was a girls' school situated a mile from the town on the Dublin road. The physical state of the building was decrepit. Dr Beaufort, whose report of his visits to the individual schools was published in 1809, said, 'The buildings are old and much out of repair, the windows are for the most part rotten and the top part of the chimneys in a ruinous state', the infirmary, 'a miserable damp room'.[52] Sixty girls were resident in the school at the time of this report. As to their education he states that the 'children read well for their age', 'they are taught to read in the Psalter, Testament and Bible, at their daily lessons and in Mrs Hannah Moore's tract as a reward' and 'they appear to be well instructed but their progress has been impeded by the prevalence of opthalmia.'[53] The books read in the Charter School in Loughrea were titles recommended in the rules of the Society. Twenty-five titles are listed in the rules and all are of a religious nature except for six titles covering spelling, reading, and arithmetic.[54] Dr Beaufort also stated that the children 'know their catechism very well, but have made no great proficiency in the explanation of it yet'. The rote learning of the time did little to enhance the understanding of what was being learnt off by heart.

At the end of their time in the Charter school, pupils were apprenticed to a Protestant master. The Charter Society gave books to the children to take with them on their apprenticeship. The books to be given were, 'one octavo *Bible*, one *Common Prayer Book* with *Companion to the Altar*, one of *Seeker's*

Lectures with sermons against Popery, one *Whole duty of man*, one of *Mann's Gospels* with notes, one of *Hannah Moore's tracts*.[55] Again the main emphasis was on reading for religious instruction and not for pleasure! The *First report of the commissioners of Irish education inquiry* in 1825[56] was very critical of the Charter schools and other visitors to the schools had detailed wretched conditions and abuses of the pupils. By this time the Charter school in Loughrea had closed down. Lecky said that they left 'a legacy of bitterness hardly equalled by any portion of the penal code.'[57]

The Charter schools only attracted a small number of the pupils being educated and the vast majority of children went to the other types of schools. These were the schools supported by patrons or societies or the pay schools. The 1826 Parochial Returns[58] mention 17 schools in Loughrea. Few details of the curriculum provided in these schools survive. The 1826 Returns merely record whether or not Scripture was read in the schools and we can see that in most of the schools it was not. Scripture was read in Pigott's Lane School and Patrick Clarke's school in Bride Street, 'not read' in four schools, 'not stated' in 10 schools and, curiously, 'read privately by one protestant child' in Miss Mullery's school in Main Street, a school of 15 pupils, of whom 12 were Catholic and three were Protestant. We can presume that the curriculum of the pay schools in Loughrea was not substantially different to other hedge or pay schools. The basic three Rs of reading, writing and arithmetic would have been taught and other subjects depending on the ability of the master or mistress. The reading material of the pay schools was as varied as the reading material available in the homes of the pupils. The shortage of books meant that pupils brought into school whatever they could lay their hands on and the easiest reading material to hand for many pupils were the chapbooks. The content of these readers in the hedge schools alarmed many and they feared for the morality of pupils exposed to such literature. The books being used in the hedge schools were one of the main reasons societies such as the Kildare Place Society embarked on massive schemes of book production. The Association for Discountenancing Vice and Promoting the Knowledge and Practice of the Christian Religion, published the tracts of Hannah More, hoping they would replace the chapbooks which the society believed were of 'the most immoral kind and inculcated principles the most pernicious'.[59] A list of the all the books found in the pay schools of four counties, Donegal, Kildare, Kerry and Galway, was published in the *First report of the commissioners of education enquiry* in 1825.[60] Ninety-two books were classified as of a *religious* nature and 292 as *works of entertainment, histories, tales etc.* McManus points out that of the 391 books listed, 'only a dozen came in for repeated criticism by education commissioners, evangelicals and conservative groups in Irish society.'[61] The vast majority of the literature read in the pay schools was the popular literature of the time and included titles such as *Don Quixote,*

BIOGRAPHICAL SKETCHES B/O

OF

EMINENT BRITISH POETS

CHRONOLOGICALLY ARRANGED

FROM CHAUCER TO BURNS,

WITH CRITICISMS ON THEIR WORKS, SELECTED FROM THE MOST DISTINGUISHED WRITERS.

INTENDED FOR TEACHERS AND THE HIGHER CLASSES IN SCHOOLS

REVISED AND PUBLISHED BY DIRECTION OF THE

No species of writing seems more worthy of cultivation than Biography, since none can be more delightful or more useful, nor can more certainly enchain the heart by irresistible interest, or more widely diffuse instruction to every diversity of condition.—JOHNSON.

Sold to Pupils in National Schools at 6d. each

DUBLIN:

BROWNE & NOLAN, LTD., 24 & 25, NASSAU-STREET.

LONDON; SIMPKIN, MARSHALL, & Co.

1907

Irish National School Books.

5. Cover and title page of Commissioners of Education text book

Tristram Shandy, Dean Swift's letters, Paradise lost, Dr. Johnson's classical essays and *Gulliver's travels*. It also included the questionable tales of robbers and high-waymen, *Captain Freney, the robber,* the *Life of Redmond O'Hanlon, the robber* and, no doubt even worse, the *Life of Lady Lucy.*

Whereas the pay schools had no standardized curriculum and no set texts to follow, the schools set up under the national system of education rigorously controlled what was read in the classroom. The Commissioners of Education were meticulous in supplying books to the national schools whose content would be acceptable to all religious denominations. They used the books of the Kildare Place Society, with agreed modifications, and those of the Catholic Book Society until books produced by the Commissioners themselves were available in 1833.[62] The readers produced by the Commissioners were not compulsory, but they were almost univer-sally used. Schools could not use other books 'unless they had been reported to and sanctioned by the Board.'[63] A first stock of the commissioners books were issued free to all schools and others could be purchased at a reduced cost.[64] However, as well as a problem of content, quantity was another issue to be tackled. The problem of a shortage of books in national schools persisted for many years after the foundation of the national system. Patrick Kelly estimated the supply of books was unsatisfactory in many schools as late as 1870.[65] In Connacht, the teachers in 95% of the schools bought books themselves from the Board and resold them to the pupils.[66] Kelly explains that because of the shortage of books and because the free stock was inadequate for the needs of many schools, books used prior to the school joining the national system were used for some time.[67]

One further element introduced by the national school system was a difference in the curriculum for boys and girls and this is reflected in the readers produced by the Commissioners. In the pay schools which preceded the national system, boys and girls were likely to follow a similar course of instruction, possibly due as much to the physical conditions as to a philosophy of education. Harford and Raftery state that 'the formal curriculum was the most powerful way in which the system of education was shaped along gendered lines'.[68] The earliest text by the Commissioners exclusively for girls was *The reading book for use of female schools* produced in 1854. *Girls reading book for the use of schools* followed in 1864. Harford and Raftery conclude that the content of these books demonstrate that the education system was to prepare girls 'for life in the domestic sphere, as carers, helpers, mothers and wives'.[69] In an analysis of gender themes in pre-1900 national school readers produced by the Commissioners and the Christian Brothers, Mac Suibhne concurs. He points to a number of conclusions: domestic and family themes are prominent in the reading books for girls but not in the reading books for boys; there is a greater emphasis on historical themes in the books for boys and mixed classes than in the books for girls and the allocation of page space to the domestic and family themes is totally confined to the reading books for girls.[70]

The reading room, local newspaper and schools were vital agents in the spread of a print culture and by the latter part of the 19th century print had become an essential part of the commercial and business life of Loughrea. The occupations listed in the trade directories show how businesses using print were becoming an integral part of the working life of the townspeople. The 1824 *Pigot's directory*[71] lists four occupations whose work, one could argue, directly required literacy skills and depended on a print environment; the apothecary, attorney, bookseller, and physician. In *Slater's directory* of 1894,[72] there were eight such occupations, agent, auctioneer, excise officer, medical officer and registrar, petty sessions clerk, physician, printer/bookseller and solicitor. That is a relatively crude way of showing that occupations totally dependent on the accessibility of print and literacy were growing through the century. In reality however, literacy and print were necessary for the running of any commercial business in the latter part of the nineteenth century. In Loughrea, the number of merchants almost doubled between 1824 and 1894. *Pigot's directory* of 1824 lists 46 merchants; 10 grocers, 21 publicans, 3 wine and spirit merchants, 1 timber merchant, 4 linen and woollen drapers, 2 earthenware dealers and 4 leather sellers. The 1894 *Slater's Directory* lists 89 such merchants; 58 grocers, 13 drapers, nine shopkeepers, 3 glass and china dealers, 2 hardware dealers and 1 each of wool merchant, bookseller, clothes dealer, leather seller. The commercial transactions of these businesses required the existence of a print culture, as did bank and post office services. Banking was established in the town by the mid century. The National Bank of Ireland opened in 1836[73] and the Dublin Banking Company was established by 1848. By 1870 the Dublin Banking Company had been replaced by the Hibernian Bank.[74] There was little in the business life of Loughrea by the end of the 19th century that did not depend upon a literate population using print for commercial transactions.

The increase in the business of the postal service demonstrates one use to which literacy and print were being put. A postal service was available in Loughrea as early as 1638 as part of the Dublin–Galway post delivery and a post office was established shortly thereafter. Letter Carriers were appointed in Connacht in the 1830s and one was appointed to Loughrea in 1836. But it was after the introduction of the Penny Post in 1840 that the numbers using the postal service increased substantially. O'Connor notes 'it brought the letter post within the reach of the less affluent sectors of the population, a factor which soon resulted in a tremendous increase in the volume.'[75] In 1839, the number of letters delivered in Ireland was 8,301,904. In 1841, it had increased to 20,794,297 and by 1855 the number had increased to 41,832,834, a five-fold increase in 16 years. Even the smaller towns of Co. Galway were increasing the volume of their business using the postal system. In 1857, Thomas Kelly was calling for the upgrading of the mail delivery between Loughrea and Woodford, where one of the businesses 'has a larger correspondence than many traders in places of much greater magnitude.'[76] With the rapid growth in correspondence, additional posting facilities were required and post boxes appeared for the first time. Loughrea got its first post box in Bride Street in 1882.[77] With the increasing numbers of literate citizens, greater outlets and uses for that literacy emerged. The amount of book packets, exclusive of newspapers, was 1,400,000 per annum in London in 1855, an increase of more than 1,000,000 on the previous year.[78] Book packets included tradesmen circulars and catalogues and it is very likely that many of those found their way to Loughrea. Catalogues for the fashionable clothes shops in Dublin could be compared with the latest arrivals in Stratton's in Main Street. Kelly noted in his diary, 'a large supply of samples by post from Jorden and Co., stationery, etc, Dublin, an order sent them'. In 1857, the *Journal* advertised that 'persons residing in the country, who subscribe to the Dublin *Family Herald*, will receive a copy of the *Dublin Advertising Gazette*, gratis enclosed in the same wrapper.'[79]

By the end of the 19th century print had become part of the fabric of Loughrea life. The demand for print from an increasingly literate population was being addressed from the many sources outlined above. But as demand was being met, so it grew. For example, the estimated number of local newspapers was 65 in 1850 and this rose consistently each year thereafter. There were 102 in 1860, 111 in 1870, 125 in 1880 and 129 in 1890.[80] Supply was fuelling demand. By the end of the century the factors which ensured the nurturing of a print culture were present in Loughrea. The basic element was literacy and by the end of the century the literacy rate was 86.4% in Loughrea. Kellys Bookshop was supplying readers with books, magazines and stationary and the reading rooms were another source of printed material. There is no evidence to suggest that the reading rooms were a source of reading material for those who could not afford to buy their reading material. Kelly's reading room and the reading room of the Social and Literary Club did not have in their membership those who could not afford to buy their books; Fr O'Donovan's Club was nearer to fulfilling that function. Supplying reading material to the poorer sections of society, despite the decline in the price of newspapers and print, was still a problem to be addressed. There is a thread running through the 19th century of attempts to encourage the spread of reading through the provision of reading rooms or societies. The reading rooms were one of the important agents of supply. However, Loughrea would have to wait until 1932 to have the permanent public reading space and material provided by the public library. Although the first public library in Ireland was opened in 1701, it was only in the latter part of the 19th century that the concept of the free public library was becoming established. The first public library to open under the Public Libraries Act was Dundalk, Co. Louth, in 1858 but it was the 1880s before other libraries opened.[81] Galway County Library was established in 1926, taking over from the Carnegie Trust Committee. Loughrea was the second branch to be established outside Galway city, Ballinasloe was the first, and opened in 1932. It seems appropriate that Lady Gregory, who as a girl stood on tiptoe in Thomas Kelly's bookshop should serve on the Carnegie Committee in Galway which was charged with providing library services to the county. She was, however, critical of the 'the mass of rubbishy fiction'[82] found on the shelves, preferring instead that more 'biographies and history and travel that are more costly and difficult to obtain'[83] should be purchased.

3. Thomas Kelly, printer, publisher and bookseller

Print had entered into all aspects of daily life by the second half of the 19th century, from the leisurely reading of novels to the transaction of business to the sending of Valentine cards. Legg notes that 'to be able to read was no longer just a skill to keep a man from drink; it was an important passport to entry into the modern world.'[1] The printing and publishing business of the Kelly family in Loughrea shows two sides of the print world in provincial Ireland. The *Loughrea Illustrated Journal*, published by Thomas Kelly, shows how a locally produced journal could be used to inform, to entertain and to promote the interests of Loughrea locally and abroad. Cronin, Gilligan and Holton[2] note the importance of examining trading in the economic and social lives of local communities and Kelly's diary gives an insight into how a small provincial bookshop and printing business functioned, what printing jobs were done and what suppliers were used.

Kelly's business in Loughrea was not confined to book selling and printing. He carried a wide variety of stationery, 'post, letter, note, foolscap and copy paper,' 'mourning and plain visiting cards,' writing desks and escritoires and 'quill pens, in boxes.' He also sold pills and ointments, shaving creams, brushes, perfumery, violin strings and wallpaper. He acted as emigration and insurance agent. His diary contains countless references to the price of oats and potatoes and other local produce, for example, 'oats 14s. to 15s. per barrel. Paid 8s. 3d. for 16½ stone potatoes at 6d. per stone.'[3] Although not specifically stated in the *Journal* or his diary, it appears that he was also dealing in these goods. An examination of this business illuminates both the practical and literary sides of the print culture in Loughrea.

The *Journal* first appeared in 1857 and was printed in three different sizes over the years, 10 x 7½ in, 15 x 10 in and 10½ x 8 inches. The *Galway Vindicator* noted on the appearance of the Journal that 'this little periodical, which considering the moderate price, contains numerous neat illustrations and interesting matter, is likely to become an established favourite.'[4] A complete set of the *Journal* is not available. Dr Thomas T. O'Farrell donated a set of bound volumes of the *Journal* containing the years 1874 to 1881 to Galway Co. Library in 1931.[5] They were given to him by the Kelly's successor in the business, Miss Canavan, who had stored them in her attic.[6] Earlier issues, but not the first, are available in the National Library of Ireland which also holds the issues from January to October 1884, the final available issues.

6. Photographs of the Kelly family, brothers Thomas and Coll
and nephew Michael S. Kelly (courtesy of Mrs A. Monaghan)

The readership of the journal cannot be accurately estimated but, as with most 19th century newspapers, it was probably low by the standards of today's publications. Kinane quotes circulation figures for the 1820s for some Galway newspapers. The *Connaught Journal* had a circulation of 192 copies, Connolly's *Weekly Advertiser*, 145 copies and the *Galway Independent*, less than 100. He quotes Wheeler's figure of 547 as an average circulation for newspapers.[7] Readership figures were usually higher than the circulation figures, as newspapers and periodicals were normally read by more than the purchaser. We can, however, estimate the scope of the journal. Thomas Kelly had agents for orders and advertisements in 'Galway, Tuam, Ballinasloe, Gort, Athenry, Clifden, Mountbellew, Portumna, Woodford, Ballymoe, Dunmore, Carrick-on-Suir etc.'[8] A Mr Kirk, bookseller, with an address at Railway Terminus, Broadstone, was the Dublin subscription agent. R.J. Kelly (no relation) states that the journal 'found its way into nearly every Galway county family.'[9] In 1881 the editorial states that the circulation continues to expand 'not alone in Ireland and England, but through the States of America, Canada, Australia, and British Columbia.'[10] The *Journal* contained a section 'to correspondents', where the editor replied to submissions received and to correspondents overseas. In January 1876, it included,

> 'The Rea and Corrib shores for me' – this poem from J.J. Ryan, New York, shall have a prominent place in our February issue,
> Exile, New York – if you hand a dollar and 10 cents to Mr. J. Ryan, 312 East 12th Street, you will get a printed receipt and the journal post-free for one year.
> Mr. P. J. Higgins, Bellvue College, New York, – money order received – many thanks.[11]

Other replies went to readers in Massachusetts, Mobile, Alabama and San Francisco. It is likely that these American correspondents had Loughrea connections and were anxious to maintain the link with Loughrea that the *Journal* provided, and as such it fulfilled an important function for them. Not all overseas subscribers had Loughrea connections. The September 1857 issue includes the following entry:

> Quebec – Mr. Thaddeus J. Walsh, Supervisor of Culler's Office, Quebec, has kindly undertaken to procure subscribers for our Journal, and on a first instalment sends us the yearly subscription of eight Irishmen, whose names we shall publish in our American edition. We beg to express our warmest thanks to Mr. Walsh, the favour being enhanced by his being an utter stranger to us.[12]

The last sentence implies that overseas subscribers usually did have Loughrea connections. It is also interesting to note that an American edition of the *Journal* was published. American subscribers must have been of a sufficient number to make it worthwhile to do so. Unfortunately, I have not been able to source a copy.

The births, marriages and deaths section gives an indication of the broad geographical spread of the journal. The February 1862 issue includes a birth notice from 'Beechworth, Australia, the wife of Bartholomew Wall, Esq. late of Dublin, a son.' Another Australian birth is recorded in October 1862 to 'the wife of P.J. Martin, Esq. in Melbourne, a daughter.' A death notice taken from the *Irish World* (New York) records the death of Edmond Healy, born in Ballinakill, just a few miles from Loughrea and illustrates the traits of the birth, marriage and notices included in the *Journal*. They are taken from a foreign publication and relate to a Loughrea native or one with local connections. Other notices refer to the gentry, professional and business classes.

One entry reads 'at Beech Hill, the residence of E.C. Villiers Esq. J.P., Jane Loles, aged seventy-six, a faithful and valued servant for over 50 years'. One other entry refers to a servant in a household, again inserted by the employer, 'Margaret Davy, for many years the valued housekeeper of Mr. John Fahy, Woodberry House, Kilconnell.'[13] A death notice for Michael H. Gill, Dublin, the eminent bookseller and publisher, appeared in April 1879 as did a death notice for Mr Alfred O'Hea, 'for many years editor and part proprietor of the *Connaught Telegraph*'. The issues of the *Journal* contained numerous references to other publishers and newspaper editors throughout the country and to newspapers and periodicals published abroad, e.g. the *Irish World* (New York), the *Western Catholic* (Chicago) and the *Journal* contained many articles taken from other local newspapers, particularly the *Galway Vindicator*. Kelly maintained a constant interest in the world of publishing and printing and demonstrated a familiarity with a wide range of Irish and foreign publications.

The *Journal* consisted of central pages taken from an external source and the outer pages were produced locally. The central pages constituted the bulk of the journal and contained works of fiction and poetry, travellers' tales, historical pieces and other miscellaneous items. For the purposes of this study, the pages produced locally are the focus of most attention. In the 20th volume in January 1876, Kelly thanked those supporters and subscribers who had supported his efforts to establish in the west of Ireland, 'a periodical devoted to literature, science and art, which would be free from a political or sectarian bias.'[14] He was quoting the prospectus of the periodical and describing its purpose. How successful was he in those objectives? He was very successful in that the journal lasted for such a long time. It started in 1857 and continued for 27 years until 1884. In the early 1880s, it ceased to be published by Thomas Kelly and was published by his nephew, Michael S. Kelly. The bulk of the contents were indeed literature, science and art but also included the useful arts e.g. lace making.

While it was generally free from an overt political bias, the *Journal* had a political message. The 'tide of emigration which is draining the life blood of the land'[15] was the subject of a leading article in November 1863. In this he called for fixity of tenure and a good Landlord and Tenant bill to be passed in the next session noting that property has its rights as well as its duties. This is the most overt political statement I have noticed but it occurs in the context of a call for the improvement in conditions for the peasants of the country. It is also one of the few articles that refers to the country as a whole and not to the local circumstances of Loughrea. Col. Thomas Kelly, who was from Mountbellew, was apprenticed to Thomas Kelly in Loughrea.[16] Col. Thomas Kelly was the Fenian leader who was freed from a police van in Manchester in 1867. Those convicted of, and executed for, the murder of a policeman during that escape were Allen, Larkin and O'Brien, later known as 'the Manchester Martyrs'. After his time in Loughrea, Col. Kelly emigrated to America where he established a newspaper in Tennessee[17] and became involved with the Fenian movement. There is no evidence of a

similar political allegiance in his Loughrea namesake although the *Journal*
was established at a time in the 1850s when, as Comerford points out, the
editors of many provincial newspapers were of strong nationalist leanings
and used their newspapers to promote the nationalist cause.[18] Thomas Kelly
had a more local focus and his main interest was in the improvement and
advancement of Loughrea. In the editorial of January 1882, on the 26th
anniversary of the establishment of the *Journal*, he was happy to see his
labours 'to promote and foster everything which we consider calculated to
advance our locality has been appreciated by the public',[19] demonstrated by
their continued support of the *Journal*. The primary focus of the local input
into the journal was to lobby for change, highlight needs, berate the
inhabitants of Loughrea for deficiencies, encourage developments and be a
voice and a focus for progress in the town. In a piece entitled 'Our prospects
and how to improve them' in the November 1857 issue, he remarked that
'while other towns in the country are rapidly rising in commercial
importance, Loughrea has been sinking in the social scale.' He advocated the
setting up a board of town commissioners and noted the improvement in
Tuam since such a board was established. He suggested the holding of a
public meeting to discuss this proposal to 'resuscitate the condition of
Loughrea – a town which by the united exertions of the people and the
proprietor, might yet be made, as in days of yore, one of the most important
in the province.'[20] In May 1858, he chided the people of the town for not
supporting the re-established brewery in the town. He noted, 'in other
towns, supplied from the Loughrea Brewery, the concern is largely
patronized – but Loughrea, which should be the first to lend its aid only
observes its consistency, by being the last in any practical movement
calculated to improve the conditions of its inhabitants.'[21] He was a long time
supporter of the campaign for the rail link from Loughrea to Attymon to
join the Dublin–Galway line and the *Journal* contains many accounts
throughout the years of meetings held in the town and delegations to
Dublin in relation to this issue. In December 1882, boards of guardians
throughout the country were directed to prepare for the distribution of
relief as conditions warranted. The *Journal* commended this course of action,
commenting that 'distress is the chronic condition of the labouring classes',
but that this will not have the slightest effect on the condition on the poor.
He called for employment to be provided that would have a permanent
effect in improving their circumstances. The employment he was referring
to was, of course, the construction of the rail link to Attymon, a constant
theme of *Journal* editorials.

In 1876, Kelly congratulated the Town Commissioners on the recent
flagging of the footpaths through the principal streets and suggested
additional streets that required paving[22] and in April of 1876 he welcomed

the work being carried out in renovating the two graveyards in the town.[23] In 1881 he called on the Loughrea board of guardians to allow the press access to their meetings, as was the case in Galway and elsewhere throughout the country. He said there may be a little natural prejudice to be overcome, as the guardians were not 'accustomed to deliberate in [the] presence of the wide world as they should did they admit the representatives of the Fourth Estate.'[24] He was obviously conscious of the role of the press in society as disseminators of information and considered it an anomaly that the meetings were not open to the public. He reassured the guardians that there was nothing to fear from this and that the public would only see that affairs were being properly managed.

Following the murder of Mr Blake and Mr Ruane in 1882 outside Loughrea, the *Journal* deplored the assassinations in the strongest terms. The editorial said 'the awful event has naturally created consternation among the inhabitants of Loughrea, who denounce the fell occurrence as the emanation of evil-doers.'[25] He praised the work of Mr. Blake in his capacity as chairman of the town commissioners and as one of the guardians of the Loughrea union. He did not however comment on the reasons for, or broader political issues involved in, the outrage.

The focus of the *Journal* was not confined to the town of Loughrea. The landed families in the Loughrea area enjoyed the pursuits followed by their class in the rest of the country and the *Journal* informed its readers on their social life with several entries as follows: 'The following distinguished personages were entertained during the past week by Sir Thomas J. Burke, Bart. M.P., and Lady Burke at their mansion, Marble Hill, while enjoying the excellent sports afforded by the cock shooting on Sir Thomas's numerous and extensive preserves – the marquis of Clanricarde, Lords Clonbrock and Dunsandle, Hon Gerald Dillon'[26] and others. In two days they 'bagged over 100 brace of cocks'. Another such entry reads, 'The Shooting party at Dunsandle on 20 and 22 Dec consisted of Sir Wm. H. Gregory, Hon. A. Browne, C.H. Knox, Colonel Daly, Colonel White, Major Blake, Capt. Lowry, and W. Trousdell etc. Game shot – Pheasants (only cocks)–656, Woodcock–20, Rabbits–45, Snipe–one, Woodquests–four, Hares–four, various–two, Total, 732.[27] The dates for the Co. Galway Hunt were usually included in the *Journal*. Indications of what was to happen nationally are also evident in the numerous advertisements for auctions of the contents of big houses, stock and farm implements contained in the *Journal*.

Through the pages of the *Journal* one can see all aspects of life in Loughrea. The same page that contained the report on the Marble Hill hunting party, contained a report of the Loughrea Fuel Committee discussing poor families in receipt of coal. It reported that 'fuel is now weekly supplied to upwards of 1,800 of the poor of the district.'[28] The advertisements in the *Journal* also reflected all activities and strata of society. On the same page as Whelan's Stores advertised 'wines embracing ports, sherries, claret, champagne, Madeira etc.', 'German and American clocks, blankets, linens and a large and valuable quantity of second-hand goods'[29] were advertised in Luke Reilly's pawn office. The same issue, February 1884, that advertised Michael Kennedy's new millinery and dressmaking department, 'well stocked with the latest London and Paris fashions' also advertised the Allan Line, 'sailing fortnightly from Galway to Boston'. For those who could not afford the latest Paris fashions, or anything resembling them, the emigrant ship was an all too common option.

Regarding a religious bias, the *Journal* was not sectarian but did give extensive coverage to local religious affairs. Religious ceremonies in the Carmelite Abbey, visits of Catholic clergy to the town, professions of nuns in the Carmelite or Mercy convents and the activities of the Temperance Society were all given extensive coverage. This was common throughout the press of the time.

The literary content of the *Journal* was partly catered for by imported material but Kelly also included local literary talent. 'Estelle Dubernay' is the title of a romantic tale set in Paris, written by Lieutenant Harold McGrath Stapleton, commissioned by the *Journal* and published over two issues. The tale begins; 'A saucy, mocking sneering little fairy was Estelle Duvernay'. The author's address is given as Acton, so it is possible that he had been based with the militia in Loughrea at one time. Another commissioned work was 'The love of pleasure – the only motive', an essay by P.J.C. Monahan which appeared in the August 1881 issue. The 'to correspondents' section of the *'Journal'* included remarks on the literary efforts submitted to the editor. He could be caustic in his replies to authors, for example, 'P.L. – Your tale is barely passable; but your attempt at wit, in ridicule of your own countrymen would not be tolerated nowadays'[30] and 'The lines of Miss M—r lack the metre and ring of even passable rhyme. They are not deficient in love and sentiment, but the writer must acquire something additional before he tunes his lyre in the "Poets Corner."'[31] ' "Ode to Night" – gives some evidence of poetic genius but not sufficiently matured to claim a corner in the Journal. Our young friend would do well to read more and write less and he may yet succeed.'[32] Running through this section was the almost constant reminder to subscribers to pay overdue subscriptions, some of which were outstanding for years.

The *Journal* illuminates one obscure aspect of life in Loughrea. The role of women in the literary life of the town is almost invisible but women were certainly prominent in the economic life of Loughrea. Ann Nolan ran a stationery shop in Loughrea according to 1846 *Slater's Directory*.[33] Eliza Coen ran a confectioner's business, Mary Duffy and Margaret Hickey were grocers, and Margaret Scanlon was a wine and spirit merchant. Of the 165

Loughrea businesses listed in the 1881 *Slater's Directory*, 25 were run by women.[34] However their wider cultural role was more difficult to define although we know from census figures that female literacy rates were rising faster than male rates towards the end of the century The reading rooms, which were a feature in Loughrea from the late 1830s, did not include women in their membership. Townsend quotes one female voice bemoaning the lack of reading facilities for women in the Repeal reading rooms nationwide.[35] Kelly mentions no female subscribers to his reading room. The Social and Literary Club of the 1890s excluded females 'stating Ladies only to be invited on special occasions, soirees etc.'[36] St Brendan's Club set up by Fr O'Donovan in 1900 had a male-only membership. In keeping with the social mores of the time the place for women was in the home and this was also demonstrated in the gender bias of the books studied in the national school system as has been already noted. There is evidence of female participation in the public sphere in that a branch of the Ladies Land League was established in the town in 1881.[37] Little record of their activities survives, but a report on the arrival of Mr John P. McCarthy back to Loughrea after a two-month imprisonment, states that the members of the Ladies Land League presented Mr McCarthy with a 'very nice address.'[38] The public space for reading was not open to women but that is not to say they did not engage in the pursuit or that they were not part of the growing print culture. The August 1857 issue of the *Journal* includes a poem, 'The world is full of love', submitted by the Loughrea Female Poetical Society and is signed, 'Flora May, FPS Office, Loughrea, 1857'. The September issue includes another poem, 'I want a husband' signed by 'Prosperina' of the same society, where she complains of parental restraint and says she is scolded if she goes 'to the shop for an hour or so/ or a novel I take up to read.' Therefore she is seeking a dead mother's son, 'mother-in-law, pardon the name.'[39] The quality of the verse is questionable but it does show that women in the town were reading and writing for pleasure and that they had formed a group to do so. The general content of the *Journal* was also aimed at a female as well as male readership; articles on lace making and stories of romance were not targeted at a male audience.

The stock of books for sale in Kelly's bookshop was targeted at a literate female, as well as male, population. In 1857, it included, apart from 'bibles, testaments, missals and manuals, in variety, every style of binding', books on 'cookery, domestic economy, gardening, farming and rural affairs' and 'ladies knitting, netting and crochet instructions.'[40] The booklist printed in the February 1882 issue contains a wide variety of literature to appeal to all readers. The bulk of the titles are either titles of Irish interest or Catholic works. It includes Irish titles such as *Knocknagow*, *Essays of T. Davis*, *Rise and fall of the Irish nation*, *O'Connell's memoir of Ireland*, *Life and speeches of T.F. Meagher* and *Ballad poetry of Ireland*. The list also includes *Modern cookery* and

NEW AND REVISED LIST OF
SELECT WORKS,
For Sale at the Loughrea Journal
BOOK AND STATIONERY ESTABLISHMENT.

	s	d
Knocknagow	3	6
Story of Ireland	3	6
Modern Cookery	1	0
Works of Cowper, and of Wordsworth (each) ...	2	0
History of Ireland	3	0
Enquire Within	2	6
Twenty Years' Recollections of an Irish Police Magistrate (Porter)..	2	0
Recollections of the Last Four Popes ...	5	0
Life of the Blessed Virgin	3	0
Testimonies of The Most High	2	0
Douay Testament	1	3
Spiritual Conferences (Faber)	6	0
Creator and Creature "	6	0
Bethlehem ... "	6	0
Holy Communion (Dalgairns)	5	0
True Spouse of Christ	6	0
Victims of the Penal Law	3	6
Two Roads of Life	2	0
Furnis's Books for Children	2	0
History of the Geraldines	1	6
Essays of T. Davis	1	0
Discourses to the Young	1	6
Second and Third Books of the Society for the Preservation of the Irish Language, 4d and	0	6
Irish Writers of the Seventeenth Century ...	1	0
O'Connell's Memoir on Ireland	1	0
Catholic Belief	0	6
Catholic Library	1	4
Angel of the Altar	2	3
Ursuline Catholic Offering	2	6
Do. do. do. gilt	3	6
The Emerald Wreath	3	6
The Rector's Daughter	2	6
Trial and Trust	2	6
Catholic Keepsake	4	0
Sister Mary's Annual	3	0
Tales and Stories by Brother James ...	3	0
Catholic Souvenir	5	0
Diary of a Sister of Mercy	4	0
Dark Shadow of the Blast	2	6
Romantic Tales of Great Men	2	0
Oliver Twist	2	0
Nicholas Nickleby	2	0
Rise and Fall of the Irish Nation ...	2	0
The Songs of Ireland	0	6
National Ballads, Songs and Poems (Davis) ...	0	6
Spirit of the Nation	0	6
Ballad Poetry of Ireland (C. G. Duffy) ...	0	6
Book of Irish Ballads (D. F. McCarthy) ...	0	6
Language of Flowers	0	6
Mudfog Papers (Dickens)	2	6
Young Duke	2	0
Henrietta Temple	2	0
Riding Recollections	2	0
The Frozen Deep	2	0
Friendship (Ouida)	2	0
Harry Lorriquer	2	0
The Denounced	2	0
The Cloven Foot	2	0
Saints and Sinners	1	0
Magnall's Historical Questions	3	0
Wild Sports of the West	2	0
Life and Speeches of T. F. Meagher ...	2	0
Handy Andy	2	0
The O'Donoghue (Lever)	2	0
Her Mother's Darling	2	0
Orange Lily	2	0
Introduction to English History, new and revised edition ...	1	8

7. List of books for sale in Thomas Kelly's shop, Feb. 1882

Enquire within, a book on household management The list comprises 66 titles. Seventeen titles relate to Irish culture including history, poetry and ballads and essays. The writers of the Young Ireland movement, Thomas Davis and Charles Gavin Duffy, feature prominently in the list. Sixteen titles are of a religious nature including a *Life of the Blessed Virgin, Recollections of the last four popes, Catholic keepsake* and *Catholic souvenir.* The works of Dickens, *Oliver Twist* and *Nicholas Nickleby* and other titles such as *Henrietta Temple* and *Young Duke* represent popular literature. Twenty-six of the books cost 3s. and over. The cheapest books were 6d., the price of the Young Ireland publications *Spirit of a nation, Ballad poetry of Ireland* and others. These books had been part of the publishing venture of the Young Irelanders who had founded *The Nation* newspaper. They were published with the purpose of making works relating to Irish history and culture available at a low cost. Some of the other titles of Irish interest were more expensive. *Knocknagow* and *Story of Ireland* were 3s. 6d. each. This would put such titles out of the range of many people as the average wage for an agricultural labourer in 1880 was between 9s. and 12s., a labourer's wage in rural Ireland in 1885 was between 9s. and 14s.[41] A list of titles published in February 1881 features 45 titles. Of these titles, 29 do not feature in the 1882 list. A list published in the September 1877 issue contained 37 titles, 24 of which do not appear in the other lists. This represents a substantial business where there was a sizable stock of books and where new titles were being constantly added.

The *Journal* advertised other printing and bookselling businesses. Thomas J. Connolly's Book establishment in Galway was frequently advertised. Connolly's supplied 'rare and curious books, both in English and Irish, relating to Ireland; also works in biography, travels, history, romance and general literature, school and classical books. All periodicals of the day are supplied to order.'[42] L. Hynes, High Street, Galway, Book-binding and Circulating Library was also advertised.[43] Hynes advertised 'books bound in every variety of style, to suit either the library or drawing room'. Also included in that 1857 issue is an advertisement for J. Wade, Confectioner in Williamsgate Street, Galway, 'Coffee and news-room', 'supplied with daily papers'. Wade was still advertising in the *Journal* in 1877 but at that date, the advertisement does not mention the coffee and news-room, only the confectionery business.

The *Journal* published lists of works stocked in the shop as discussed above, but also carried individual advertisements for books and journals. The first issue of the *Irish Literary Gazette*, a weekly journal, devoted to national literature, criticism, fiction, industry, science and art was advertised in September 1857. *Eason's almanac and handbook for Ireland for the year 1879* was advertised in Jan. 1879. *The Book of Common Prayer* was advertised in June 1881 in a 'new and varied selection in every style of binding varying in price from one penny, (Children's Hymnals) to five shillings'. *Tenant's key to the new land act* by T.M. Healy, MP (price 1s.) was advertised in November 1881, reflecting current concerns on the land issue.

Local businesses in Loughrea supported the *Journal* by advertising in its pages throughout its existence. Whelan's Stores and William Stratton advertised in 1862. Stratton's advertised throughout the run of the *Journal*. After the death of William Stratton in 1883, the advertisement included the information that his wife was continuing the business. The auctioneer, J. Larkin, advertised his business for many years, as did the Misses Flynn, who ran a millinery and china-ware establishment, Michael Sweeny, grocer and hardware merchant in Bride Street and P. Burke, who ran a flour and meal business. Mr Manning, photographer, also advertised in the final available issue and had been doing so for many years. Advertisements for businesses in other Galway towns also featured, John McCarthy, Draper and Haberdasher, Main Street Eyrecourt, John M. Glynn, Assorted Warehouse, Gort and of course, Moon's drapery shop in Galway. Moon's advertised black silk and velvet jackets, overskirts, crinolines, stays, feathers, flowers and ornaments, lace and muslin curtains. Businesses in Dublin advertised, such as the Commercial Hotel in Bridge Street and the European Hotel, Bolton Street as did P. Short, Great Denmark Street selling 'Porpoise hide Ladies Field and Country Boots, thoroughly waterproof and suitable for croquet, archery, riding or gardening'. Oldham's Medical Halls, Grafton Street and Dame Street, supplier of Holloways Pills, cattle and horse medicines was a constant advertiser, This was part of a wider business arrangement as Oldham also supplied Kellys with goods for sale. Throughout the printing of the *Journal*, advertisements continued for emigrant ships. Thomas Kelly himself was appointed agent in 1858 for a Liverpool Passenger Broker, James Thomas Walthew.[44] There are also numerous advertisements for insurance companies, particularly the Sun Fire Office, for which Michael S. Kelly was agent in 1881. Thomas had been agent for that company and for Sun Life Association Society prior to that. Financial services were advertised such as 'The sum of £1,500 to be lent'. This was not from a bank but from a solicitor in Dublin, John Thornton.[45]

The diary of Thomas Kelly sheds light on the commercial side of his publishing business. As this was a diary and not a ledger or cashbook, there is no way of knowing if this was the full extent of his transactions although it does note orders made and invoices paid to wholesalers. A typical entry reads, 'Day rather fine. Two chests goods from E. Heley's ordered from Mr. Lawless three weeks hence – variety of ink stands, pencils, note paper, envelopes etc., invoice £23 12s. 10d.' (Tuesday 21 February 1860) or 'Yesterday and today a great improvement in the weather and consequently all hands are at work. A large parcel of national school books from J. Falconer, 53, Upper Sackville Street, Dublin. Invoice £1 10s. 4d. less 4s. 6d. discount' (Monday 5 March 1860). Most entries start with a weather report,

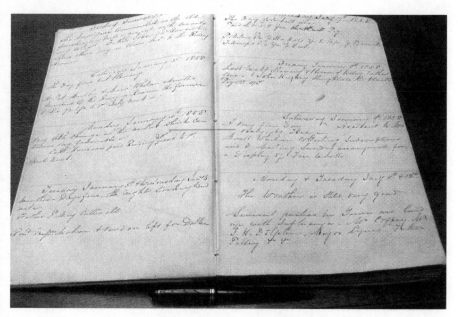

8. Pages from the Diary of Thomas Kelly

understandable in a society where suitable weather conditions were vital for the success of crops essential to the local economy. But the short, often terse, entries give a glimpse of contemporary life in provincial Ireland. The entry for 14 June 1860 notes 'the greater part of the day occupied in booking passengers for America, the *Golden-Fleece* to sail on 23rd inst. and the *Pazana* on 26th inst.' There are numerous entries mentioning the travelling salesmen who called to his shop. Mr Lawless from Heleys is mentioned frequently. The diary covers the period 1858 to 1863. Entries for 1862 and 1863 are infrequent whereas 1858 to 1861 contain almost daily entries.

The diary for 1859 is a snapshot of one year's trading and it gives the picture of a busy enterprise. His biggest supplier was Richardsons, the printers and publishers, Thomas Richardson and Son, Capel St, Dublin. The total amount paid to this company for 1859 was £60 11s. 9½d. for two consignments of goods. During the course of the year he received three consignments from Heleys, the wholesale paper warehouse on Ormond Quay, Dublin, totalling £17 19s. 7d. The type of goods received from Heleys were, note paper, envelopes, copy and pass books, brown paper, inks. He also gets stationery from Jordans. Oldhams supplied the business with a side variety of goods; hair oil, soaps, matches, marking ink, writing ink, Holloway's pills, perfumery, soap and rat poison, for which he paid in total £47 7s. 6d. He got paper from Galway Mills, room papers from Brooks in Dublin and books from McGlashens. On 29 January he received his consignment of Valentine cards from Tallons, Henry Street, Dublin for which he paid £1 1s. 6d. He paid £2 11s. 0d. to Tallons, for violin strings. It is interesting that so much of his stock came from Dublin and so little from Galway, demonstrating that, although only 23 miles away, the city was not a dominant influence on Loughrea and was itself not a thriving provincial capital during that period.

Sixteen separate printing jobs are mentioned in Kelly's diary for 1859. Many were for the Catholic clergy. He printed the bishop's pastoral letter, 2,000 tickets for the Mercy Sisters' May fair and for the bishop, copies of the pope's letter relative to the Franco-Austrian war. He also had election related printing work, 500 copies of an address for Sir Thomas Burke and 500 posters calling an election meeting in the Fair Green. He printed 400 notices for the Militia calling in members to meet in Galway. For the drapers of the town, he printed notices informing customers that the shops would be closed on St Stephen's Day to allow shop workers an extra day off. The most intriguing order for printing was for a Mr Fitzgerald for 'circulars to be printed for the clergy of the diocese relative to the £100 he lost in the bank last week.'[46] Presumably the clergy were being asked to announce the loss and appeal for information at masses throughout the diocese. Or in light of the huge loss £100 would have been at the time, perhaps he was seeking divine intervention.

The *Journal* ceased publication in 1884, presumably with the death of Thomas Kelly. R.J. Kelly states it 'was his creature and it died with its creator'.[47] The rest of the business continued under Michael S. Kelly who died in 1903, aged 60 years. Coll Kelly, a brother of Thomas, was also involved in the business. He died in 1882 and was buried in Mountbellew. Michael S. Kelly left the business to Ann Jane Kelly. It still operates as a bookshop, newsagent and fancy goods business, but not as a printing or publishing business and without 'quill pens, in boxes'.[48]

Thomas Kelly's business was not a large one by printing and publishing standards. What makes his business worthy of study is that it gives a glimpse into how print worked in Loughrea in the latter half of the nineteenth century. The list of items for sale in his shop shows what people used in everyday correspondence. The list of books for sale gives an idea of the market for books in a provincial town in the latter half of the 19th century. The advertisements for other local businesses uniquely show what was available in those shops at that period, as advertisements for these businesses are not available in other sources. The articles written in the *Journal* show how Kelly campaigned for the improvement in the condition of the town. The *Journal* also shows that women were part of the print culture of Loughrea and books mentioned in the book lists and articles in the *Journal* were aimed at a female as well as male audience. The *Journal* has been a

9. Kelly's shop in Main Street, now 'News'n'Choose'

neglected source on the history of Loughrea but one that deserves greater attention.

Thomas Kelly's publishing business illustrates the interaction of the supply and demand for print in 19th-century Loughrea. At one level he supplied books for those who wanted to enhance their literary or theological knowledge or improve their command of cookery or gardening skills. At another, and probably more important level he was the producer of cheap print: handbills and circulars that littered the streets of Loughrea on a fair day. His own production of the *Loughrea Illustrated Journal* illustrates the importance of print to the new middle class emerging in Loughrea. For them it was the channel through which they campaigned for the much needed local improvement and the opportunity to display their new found position in polite society through reading and writing, In that sense, the *Journal* conveys the views of middle-class Loughrea in a way that local politics does not.

Conclusion

As a young girl, Lady Gregory, then Augusta Persse, stood on tiptoes in the bookshop in Loughrea buying her beloved books. Sixty years later she served on the Galway Co. Council Carnegie Libraries Committee, guiding the provision of a library service to Loughrea and the county as a whole. Loughrea public library opened in 1932 in the Temperance Hall, the same location that housed the reading room of St Brendan's Total Abstinence Society, founded by Fr Jeremiah O'Donovan in 1900. One of the main themes to emerge from this study is the presence of a continuous thread of reading and attempts at providing opportunities for reading in Loughrea in the 19th century. From the 1830s Temperance Society, through the Repeal reading room in the 1840s and Thomas Kelly's reading room of the 1850s and 1860s, to the Loughrea Social and Literary Club in the 1890s and Fr O'Donovan's Temperance Society at the turn of the century, the desire for reading facilities is evident. The reading rooms in Loughrea originated from different ideological and social reasons. The Temperance and Repeal reading rooms were part of wider national campaigns, whereas Thomas Kelly's reading room was more of a gentleman's club. Whether from ideological or social reasons, they all demonstrate the importance attached to reading and the supply of printed material within the town. It might appear that by the middle of the 19th century print culture should have been firmly established in Loughrea, but with a literacy rate of only 29% in 1851, this can hardly be claimed. Literacy rates climbed throughout the period, but there was still a 13% illiteracy rate in Loughrea by 1901.

The reading rooms mentioned above differed substantially from each other, but along with their promotion of a print culture, they shared one significant factor: they all excluded women from their membership. However, women's apparent absence from Loughrea's print culture is not the full story. While they did not partake in its public manifestations, women were taking part in a print culture at a private level. The books for sale in Kelly's bookshop, the subject matter of articles in the *Journal* and the presence of the work of local female poets in the *Journal* all demonstrate that women were active in the world of print. This is also shown by the amount of women who ran businesses in the town towards the end of the 19th century when literacy and familiarity with the world of print was an essential component of commercial activity.

Loughrea had a history of printing prior to the 19th century. This was unusual for a small town in the west of Ireland, as the west was slower to embrace printing than other parts of the country. McClintock Dix uncovered fragments of Loughrea printing dating back to 1766 and the output of print continued into the 19th century. Because of the survival of the *Journal* and Thomas Kelly's diary, it has been possible to look in detail at printing in Loughrea in the latter half of the 19th century. The *Loughrea Illustrated Journal* was published over a period of 27 years from 1857 to 1884, remarkable at a time when many local publications, particularly newspapers had short lives.[1] The *Journal* has not been used extensively as a source for local history, but for an examination of the print culture in Loughrea, it is unique. Through its pages we see Loughrea as a town struggling to improve its condition after a long period of neglect by the landlord, the earl of Clanricarde, and continuing to suffer from post-Famine population decline. Through the *Journal* we also see a town where Kelly's bookshop sold the latest published titles and also luxury items like silver penholders. We can see this contrast clearly in the advertisements in the *Journal*. The latest Paris fashions were available in Strattons drapery shop in Main Street and the nearby local pawn shop was advertising its business.

The history of provincial printing in Ireland is as yet an under-researched area. McClintock Dix has uncovered and listed much of the earliest surviving examples of provincial printing but much remains to be done. This study of Loughrea has attempted to look at the different components of print culture in an Irish provincial town: its literacy levels throughout the period, the supply of print in the form of printers and bookshops, facilities for reading in the form of reading rooms, and how print had, by the end of the nineteenth century, become part of the fabric of commercial life in the town. Other towns deserve similar attention. Tuam, Co. Galway, also has a rich history of printing, particularly of newspapers. Similar studies of other towns would provide valuable comparisons and contribute to a neglected area of Irish local studies. Studies of the latter part of the 19th century, when literacy rates increased to include the vast majority of the population, would be particularly instructive. In Ireland, there has been little examination of this theme or of its importance for local communities or at national level.

Notes

ABBREVIATIONS

HC   House of Commons
LIJ   The Loughhrea Illustrated Journal
JGAHS   Journal of the Galway Archaeological and Historical Society
UCD   University College Dublin

INTRODUCTION

1 LIJ, 1 Aug. 1857.
2 Raymond Gillespie, Reading Ireland (Manchester, 2005), p. vi.
3 Roger Chartier, The culture of print (Cambridge, 1989), p. 1.
4 E.R. McClintock Dix, 'Early Loughrea printing' in JGAHS, 4:2 (1905–6), 110–12 and 'Earliest Loughrea printing' in JGAHS, 5:3 (1907–8), 194–5.
5 Gerard Long (ed.), Books beyond the pale: aspects of the provincial book trade in Ireland before 1850 (Dublin, 1996).
6 Bernadette Cunningham and Máire Kennedy (eds), The experience of reading: Irish historical perspective (Dublin, 1999).
7 Lawrence McBride (ed.), Reading Irish histories: texts, contexts, and memory in modern Ireland (Dublin, 2003).
8 Mary Daly and David Dickson (eds), The origins of popular literacy in Ireland: language change and educational development, 1700–1920 (Dublin, 1990).
9 Niall Ó Ciosáin, Print and popular culture in Ireland, 1750–1850 (Basingstoke, 1997).
10 Antonia McManus, The Irish hedge school and its books, 1695–1831 (Dublin, 2004).
11 Donald H. Akenson, The Irish education experiment (London, 1970).
12 Marie-Louise Legg, Newspapers and nationalism: the Irish provincial press, 1850–1892 (Dublin, 1999).
13 Mary Casteleyn, A history of literacy and libraries in Ireland (Aldershot, 1984).
14 Joseph Forde, Christina Cassidy, Paul Manzor and David Ryan (eds), The district of Loughrea, vol. 1: history 1791–1918 (Loughrea, 2003).
15 Mary Feeney, 'Print for the people: the growth in popular writings and reading facilities in Ireland, 1820–1850' (M.Litt. thesis, UCD, 1982).
16 Michael Fahy, 'Education in Loughrea and its environs to 1861' (M.Ed. thesis, UCG, 1988).
17 John Logan, 'Schooling and the promotion of literacy in nineteenth-century Ireland' (PhD thesis, UCC, 1992).
18 John O'Donovan, Letters containing information relative to the antiquities of the county of Galway, vol. II, reproduced under the direction of the Revd M. O'Flanagan (Bray, 1928), p. 71.
19 Ibid., p. 73.
20 Ibid., p. 78.
21 Phelim Monahan, The Carmelite abbey, Loughrea, Co. Galway, 1645–1983 (Loughrea, no date), p. 9.
22 Peter Harbison, A thousand years of church heritage in east Galway (Dublin, 2005), pp 117–24.

23 See table 3.
24 *Parliamentary gazetteer* (2 vols, Dublin, 1846), ii, p. 697.
25 Pádraig Ó Cuimín, 'The Loughrea to Attymon railway' in Forde et al., (eds), *The district of Loughrea, vol. 1*, p. 419.
26 *Royal Commission on Labour: the agricultural labourer*, vol iv, Ireland, pt III, HC 1893, [6894], xx, p. 23.
27 *Second report of the commissioners of Irish education inquiry*, HC 1826–7 (12), xii, p.1220
28 *Dublin Penny Journal*, 2, No. 89 (1834).

1. THE DEMAND FOR PRINT IN
LOUGHREA

1 Timothy P. O'Neill, 'Minor famine and relief in county Galway, 1815–1925' in Gerard Moran (ed.), *Galway: history and society* (Dublin, 1996), p. 446.
2 John Cunningham, 'A spirit of self-preservation', in Joseph Forde et al. (eds), *The district of Loughrea, vol. 1* (Loughrea, 2003), p. 459.
3 Ibid., p. 458.
4 *Royal Commission on Labour: the agricultural labourer*, vol. iv, Ireland, pt III, HC 1893, [6894], xx, p. 5.
5 James P. Murray, 'A lesser-known famine crisis in Galway 1879/80' in *Journal of the Galway Family History Society*, 4 (1996–7), 94.
6 *The agricultural labourer*, p. 23.
7 Ibid., p. 22.
8 *Parliamentary gazetteer* (2 vols, Dublin, 1846), ii, p. 697.
9 *The agricultural labourer*, p. 13.
10 Hely Dutton, *A statistical survey of the County Galway* (Dublin, 1824) pp 328–9.
11 Ibid., p. 411.
12 *LIJ*, 1 Jun 1857.
13 Samuel Maguire, 'Galway profiles' in the *Galway Reader*, 1:3 (Winter 1948), 36–7.
14 Ibid.
15 Robert S. Fortner, 'The culture of hope and the culture of despair: the print media and 19th-century Irish emigration', *Eire-Ireland*, 13:3 (Fall 1978), 43.
16 Ó Ciosáin, *Print and popular culture in Ireland*, p. 27.
17 Quoted in Kevin Whelan, 'The republic in the village' in Gerard Long (ed.), *Books beyond the Pale: aspects of the provincial book trade in Ireland before 1850* (Dublin, 1996) p. 103.
18 David Ryan, 'Disaffection and rebellious conspiracy in the Loughrea area 1791–1804' in Forde et al., *The district of Loughrea, vol. 1*, p. 17.
19 Ibid., p. 31.
20 Stephen Randolph Gibbons, *Captain Rock, night errant: the threatening letters of pre-famine Ireland* (Dublin, 2004), p. 163.
21 Ibid., p. 40.
22 Charles Gavin Duffy, *Young Ireland: a fragment of Irish history* (London, 1880), p. 388
23 Whelan, 'The republic in the village', p. 105.
24 Logan, 'Schooling and the promotion of literacy', pp 223–4.
25 Ibid., p. 223.
26 *Twenty-second detailed annual report of the Registrar-General (Ireland); containing a general abstract of the numbers of marriages, births and deaths registered in Ireland during the year 1885*, p. 9 [C4801], HC 1886, xvii.701.
27 *Seventeenth detailed annual report of the Registrar-General of marriages, births and deaths in Ireland, 1880*, p. 6 [C.3046], HC 1881, xxvII.879.
28 *Slater's national commercial directory of Ireland* (Manchester, 1870), p. 50.
29 R.B. McDowell, *The Irish administration, 1801–1914* (London, 1964), p. 283 quoted in E. Margaret Crawford, *Counting the people* (Dublin, 2003), p. 20.
30 Sr Majella O Keefe, 'The workhouse system in Loughrea', 1846–51 in Forde et al., *District of Loughrea*, p. 197.
31 *Census of Ireland, 1901*, pt I: *Area, houses, and population: also the ages,*

civil or conjugal condition, occupations, birthplaces, religion, and education of the people, vol iv, *province of Connaught,* no. 1, *county of Galway,* [Cd 1059] H.C. 1902, p. 244.

32 J.R.R. Adams, *The printed word and the common man* (Belfast, 1987), p. 163.

2. THE SUPPLY OF PRINT IN LOUGHREA

1 Raymond Gillespie, *Reading Ireland* (Manchester, 2005), p. 88.
2 W.G. Wheeler, 'The spread of provincial printing in Ireland up to 1850', *Irish Booklore,* 4:1 (1978), 9.
3 Vincent Kinane, 'The early book trades in Galway' in Gerard Long (ed.), *Books beyond the Pale: aspects of the provincial book trade in Ireland before 1850* (Dublin, 1996), pp 54–5.
4 E.R. Mc Clintock Dix, 'Earliest Loughrea printing' in *Journal of the Galway Archaeological and Historical Society,* 5 (1911), 195.
5 'A Loughrea printer' in *Irish book lover,* 17:5 (Sept.–Oct., 1929), 120.
6 Ó Ciosáin, *Print and popular culture,* p. 52.
7 Wheeler, 'The spread of provincial printing', p. 7.
8 McClintock Dix, 'Early Loughrea printing', p. 111.
9 J. Pigot, *The commercial directory of Ireland, Scotland and the four most northern counties of England for 1820–1 and 1822* (Manchester, 1824), p. 210.
10 *LIJ,* 1 Aug 1877.
11 Ibid.
12 Wheeler, 'The spread of provincial printing', p. 14.
13 Feeney, 'Print for the people', p. 17.
14 Ibid., p. 7.
15 Earl of Rosse to Lord Redesdale, 19 Apr. 1822, quoted in Samuel Clark and James S. Donnelly Jr (eds), 'Pastorini and Captain Rock: millenarianism and sectarianism in the Rockite movement of 1821–1824' in *Irish peasants: violence and political unrest, 1780–1914* (Manchester, 1983), p. 111.

16 Feeney, 'Print for the people', p. 127.
17 Speech by Charles Gavin Duffy, *Freeman's Journal,* 5 Oct. 1841 quoted in Paul Townsend 'Academies of nationality: the reading room and Irish national movements, 1838–1905' in McBride (ed.), *Reading Irish histories,* p. 24.
18 *Tuam Herald,* 15 Aug. 1840.
19 *LIJ,* 1 Dec. 1875.
20 Ibid., 1 April 1876.
21 *Slater's Commercial Directory of Ireland, 1881* (Manchester, 1881) p. 55.
22 *Tuam Herald,* 25 Jan. 1845.
23 Ibid., 1 Feb. 1845.
24 *Galway Vindicator,* 12 Apr. 1845.
25 Ibid.
26 Minutes of Loughrea Social and Literary Club in Christine Cassidy, 'Loughrea Social & Literary Club' in Forde et al., *District of Loughrea,* p. 443.
27 Thomas Kelly diary, 7 Jan. 1860.
28 Ibid., 10 July 1862.
29 Ibid., 25 July 1860.
30 Ibid., 10 Sept. 1860.
31 Minutes of the Loughrea Social and Literary Club, no date (Galway County Library, Galway Co. Council Archives).
32 Ibid., 25 Aug. 1892.
33 John F. Ryan, 'Gerald O'Donovan: priest, novelist and Irish revivalist' in *JGAHS,* 48 (1996), 16.
34 Ibid., p. 7.
35 Ibid. p. 14.
36 George William Russell, 'Village Libraries' in *Selections from the contributions to the* Irish Homestead *by G.W. Russell—Æ,* Vol. 1 (Gerards Cross, 1978) p. 80.
37 Ibid.
38 Alexis de Tocqueville, *Journeys to England and Ireland* (London, 1958), p. 167.
39 Marie-Louise Legg, *Newspapers and nationalism; the Irish provincial press, 1850–1892* (Dublin, 1999), p. 172.
40 Diary of Thomas Kelly, 28 Aug. 1858.
41 Ibid., 8 Sept. 1859.
42 Ibid., 7 June 1859.
43 Ibid., 28 June 1859.

44 *Galway Vindicator*, 12 Apr. 1845.
45 Diary of Thomas Kelly, 18 June
    1859.
46 Ibid., 25 Aug. 1859.
47 Quoted in Raymond Gillespie,
    Reading Ireland, p. 66.
48 Lady Gregory, *Seventy years: being the
    autobiography of Lady Gregory* (New
    York, 1976), p. 4.
49 Ibid., p.15.
50 Ibid., p. 13.
51 *Third Report from the Commissioners
    of the Board of Education in Ireland*,
    HC 1809 (142), vii, p.16.
52 Ibid., Appendix no 7, p. 69
53 Ibid.
54 Ibid., Appendix No. 3, Books used
    in the Protestant Charter Schools,
    p. 40.
55 Ibid., Appendix No. 5, p. 51.
56 *First report of the commissioners of
    education inquiry*, HC 1825 (400), xii.
57 W.E.H. Lecky, *History of Ireland in
    the eighteenth century*, i (London,
    1913), p. 234, quoted in Antonia
    McManus, *Irish hedge school and its
    books* (Dublin 2004), p. 1.
58 *Second report of the commissioners of
    Irish education inquiry*, HC 1826–7,
    (12), xii, p. 1220.
59 McManus, *Irish hedge-school and its
    books*, p. 12.
60 *First report of the commissioners of
    education enquiry*, HC 1825, (400),
    xii, 1. App. No. 221, pp 553–9,
    quoted in McManus, *The Irish
    hedge-school and its books*, p. 12.
61 McManus, *The Irish hedge-school and
    its books*, p. 12.
62 Akenson, *The Irish education
    experiment*, p. 228.
63 *First report of the commissioners*, p. 4.
64 Ibid.
65 Patrick V. Kelly, 'The national
    system of education in Connacht,
    1831–1870' (MA thesis, UCD,
    1975), p. 166.
66 Ibid.
67 Ibid., p. 167.
68 Judith Harford and Deirdre Raftery,
    'The education of girls within the
    national system' in Deirdre Raftery
    and Susan M. Parkes, *Female

    education in Ireland, 1700–1900*
    (Dublin, 2007), p. 40.
69 Ibid., p. 44.
70 Seosamh Mac Suibhne, *Oblivious to
    the dawn: gender themes in 19th century
    national school reading books, Ireland,
    1831–1900* (Sligo, 1996), pp 78–82.
71 J. Pigot, *The commercial directory of
    Ireland, Scotland and the four most
    northern counties of England for
    1820–1 and 1822* (Manchester, 1824),
    pp 210–11.
72 *Slater's commercial directory of Ireland*
    (Manchester, 1894), pp 74–5.
73 G.L. Barrow, *The emergence of the
    Irish banking system, 1820–1856*
    (Dublin, 1975), p. 216.
74 Both the Hibernian and National
    banks, in their amalgamated forms
    of Bank of Ireland and Allied Irish
    Bank, remain in the town today.
75 Jimmy O'Connor, 'Aspects of
    Galway postal history 1638–1984',
    in *JGAHS*, 44 (1992), 140.
76 *LIJ*, 1 June 1857.
77 Jimmy O'Connor, 'Aspects of
    Galway postal history', 154
78 The post office, *Irish Quarterly
    Review*, 23:6 (1856), 521.
79 *LIJ*, 1 Sept. 1857.
80 Legg, *Newspapers and nationalism*, pp
    30, 77, 125.
81 Mary Casteleyn, *A history of literacy
    and libraries in Ireland* (Aldershot,
    1984), pp 176–7.
82 Lady Gregory, *Lady Gregory's
    journals; volume two, books thirty to
    forty-four, 21 February 1925–9 May
    1932* (New York, 1974), p. 36.
83 Ibid., p. 39.

3. THOMAS KELLY, PRINTER,
PUBLISHER AND BOOKSELLER

1 Legg, *Newspapers and nationalism*,
   p. 175.
2 Denis A. Cronin, Jim Gilligan &
   Karina Holton (eds), *Irish fairs and
   markets: studies in local history*
   (Dublin, 2001), p. 13.
3 Diary of Thomas Kelly, 24 June 1858.
4 *Galway Vindicator*, 11 Feb. 1857.

5 Minutes of the Galway County Council Carnegie Library Committee, 20 April 1931 (Galway County Council Archives).

6 Thomas T. O'Farrell, 'The Loughrea Journal', *Irish Book Lover*, 19 (Nov./Dec. 1931), 172.

7 Vincent Kinane, 'The early book trades in Galway', in Long (ed.), *Books beyond the Pale*, p. 64.

8 *LIJ*, 1 Oct. 1857.

9 R.J. Kelly, 'Later printing in Loughrea' *Irish Book Lover*, 2 (1972), 181.

10 *LIJ*, 1 Jan. 1882.

11 *LIJ*, 1 Jan. 1876.

12 *LIJ*, 1 Sept. 1857.

13 *LIJ*, 1 Feb. 1879.

14 *LIJ*, 1 Jan. 1876.

15 *LIJ*, 1 Nov. 1863.

16 Paul Rose, *The Manchester martyrs* (London, 1970), p. 18

17 Ibid., p. 18.

18 R.V. Comerford, *The Fenians in context: Irish politics & society, 1848–1882* (Dublin, 1985), p. 45.

19 *LIJ*, 1 Jan. 1882.

20 *LIJ*, 1 Nov. 1857.

21 *LIJ*, 1 May 1858.

22 *LIJ*, 1 Feb. 1876.

23 *LIJ*, 1 Apr. 1876.

24 *LIJ*, 1 Aug. 1881

25 *LIJ*, 1 July 1882.

26 *LIJ*, 1 Feb. 1862.

27 *LIJ*, 1 Dec. 1877.

28 *LIJ*, 1 Feb. 1862

29 *LIJ*, 1 Feb. 1862.

30 *LIJ*, I Sept. 1879.

31 *LIJ*, 1 Mar. 1882.

32 *LIJ*, 1 Jun. 1857.

33 *Slater's Directory of Ireland, 1846,* (Manchester, 1846), p. 130.

34 *Slater's Commercial Directory of Ireland, 1881* (Manchester, 1881), pp 53–5.

35 Paul Townsend, 'Academies of nationality: the reading room and Irish national movements, 1838–1905' in McBride (ed.), *Reading Irish histories*, p. 34.

36 Minutes of the Loughrea Social and Literary Club, 25 Sept. 1892 (MS in Galway County Library).

37 *LIJ*, 1 Apr. 1881.

38 *LIJ*, 1 Nov. 1881

39 *LIJ*, 1 Sept. 1857.

40 *LIJ*, 1 Sept. 1857.

41 *LIJ*, p. 321.

42 *LIJ*, p. 321.

43 *LIJ*, 1 June 1857

44 *LIJ*, 1 Mar. 1858.

45 *LIJ*, 1 Apr. 1877.

46 Diary of Thomas, 22 Oct. 1859 (unpublished, in private hands)

47 R.J. Kelly, 'The Loughrea Journal', *Irish Book Lover*, 2 (June 1911), 181.

48 Mrs Ann Monaghan (*née* Kelly), a niece of Miss Canavan, ran the business before it was sold in the early 1990s.

CONCLUSION

1 Short-lived local newspapers of the 19th century included: *Connacht People and Ballinsloe Independent,* 1884–6, *Western Argus,* 1828–33, *Galway Independent* 1929–32, *Galway Standard,* 1842–3.